WATERLOO

WATERLOO

JOHN NAYLOR

"He used to say that he was accustomed to read so
many conflicting descriptions of the battle that he would soon
begin to believe he was not there himself"

SIR HERBERT MAXWELL: *The Life of Wellington*

LONDON

B. T. BATSFORD LTD

First published, 1960
Second impression, 1960

MADE AND PRINTED IN GREAT BRITAIN BY
WILLIAM CLOWES AND SONS LTD, LONDON AND BECCLES
FOR THE PUBLISHERS
B. T. BATSFORD LTD
4 FITZHARDINGE STREET, PORTMAN SQUARE, LONDON, W.1

PREFACE

Although Wellington's army at Waterloo was an allied force in which the British contingent was outnumbered by troops from other countries, I have generally thought it convenient to follow the long-established practice of referring to it as the English army. The narrative itself should establish the contributions made by the foreign contingents and by the non-English regiments from the United Kingdom. The chapters which discuss armament, tactics and the life of the soldier are concerned with the English army proper.

I have felt that the presence of source references in the text would only appear pretentious in a book with negligible claims to scholarship and none to original research. A few works have contributed so largely to this account of Waterloo that they deserve mention outside the bibliography. Several chapters have been strongly influenced by Major-General J. F. C. Fuller's masterly analysis of the campaign in his *Decisive Battles of the Western World*, and I have drawn a good deal of the factual material from Henri Houssaye's monumental *1815*. In the first part of this book I am considerably indebted to General Jean Regnault's notable article on contemporary tactics in the *Revue Historique de l'Armée* of September 1951, and to his original and authoritative study: *La Campagne de 1815: Mobilisation et Concentration*. My thanks are due to Commandant Henry Lachouque for his great kindness in allowing me to base the two battlefield plans on those he published recently in *Le Secret de Waterloo*. Although I have profited greatly from the advice and encouragement of General Regnault and Commandant Lachouque throughout this book, they are not, of course, to be considered responsible for any opinion it may contain.

I should like to express my appreciation of the help I have received from the staff of the British Museum Reading Room and the Librarian of Camberwell Public Libraries. Finally, I am extremely grateful to my wife, and to Mr. Brian Southam, of Lincoln College, Oxford, for their revision of the text.

CONTENTS

LIST OF ILLUSTRATIONS

9

LIST OF ILLUSTRATIONS

ACKNOWLEDGMENT

The author and publishers wish to thank the following for
permission to reproduce the illustrations included in this book:
His Grace the Duke of Leeds, for fig. 1; Wing Commander
T. H. Lucas, for fig. 26; The Trustees of the British Museum,
for figs. 21, 22, 25 and 34; National Portrait Gallery, for fig. 1;
The Parker Gallery, for fig. 20; Radio Times Hulton Picture
Library, for figs. 17 and 19; The Trustees of the Victoria and
Albert Museum, for figs. 2, 3, 13, 16, 18, 23, 24 and 29–33.

I

Preparations for War

ON THE 4TH OF MAY, 1814, Napoleon landed on the Isle of Elba.
Bidding farewell to the Imperial Guard at Fontainebleau a few
weeks before, he had told them that henceforth he would devote
himself to describing the great deeds he and they had accomplished
together; within three days of his arrival on the island he had already
made an exhaustive tour of inspection and drawn up plans of
reform. He had begun his exile with the same energy with which
he had governed his Empire for so many years; but in a realm of
20,000 acres, it was the appearance and not the reality of activity.
He was forty-four, and in excellent health. "I have never seen",
wrote Sir Neil Campbell, the English Commissioner, on the 27th
of May,

> "a man in any situation of life with so much personal activity
> and restless perseverance. He appears to be so gratified by
> perpetual movement and in seeing those who accompany him
> sink under fatigue (which has been the case on several occasions
> where I have accompanied him), that I do not think it possible
> for him to sit down to study, or pursuits of retirement, as
> proclaimed by him to be his intention, so long as his state of
> health permits corporal exercise. After being yesterday on
> foot in the heat of the sun from 5 a.m. until 3 p.m., visiting the
> frigates and transports even in the hold among the horses, he
> rode on horseback for three hours, as he told me afterwards,
> 'pour se défatiguer'."

For the first few months there was no thought of a return to
France, of which the Emperor's last memories were the defection
of the Marshals, led by Ney, and the abuse of the crowds in the
royalist south, whose hostility had obliged him to complete the
last stages of his journey in disguise. The news which began to
filter through from the mainland helped to salve Napoleon's

wounded pride. Louis XVIII had been away from France for twenty years* and his government was faced with more than the problem of putting back the clock as far as it seemed safe or even possible to do: not all the bonapartist administrators could be dismissed, not all the holders of national lands could be dispossessed, not all the returned exiles could receive the rewards they felt their due; the Restoration had the ungrateful task of dismantling a war machine which had absorbed the efforts of France for nearly a quarter of a century. In the first place it was impossible to maintain an army of half a million men in time of peace. The 12,000 officers put on half-pay provided the focus of discontent amongst the military; a captain *en demi-solde* received 73 francs each month, and a lieutenant 44 francs†. Meanwhile, to gratify the royalists' desire to get into uniform, over 300 were gazetted as generals in less than a year. Few of these officers were qualified for such high rank, and a substantial proportion sought only prestige and a sinecure; many were content to give in to the persuasion of the Ministry of War and accept purely honorary appointments. The Imperial Guard were rebaptised *chasseurs* and *grenadiers de France*, and dispersed about the country, their pay reduced by a third. Yet the unemployment and resentment of the Emperor's former soldiers would have been a matter of small importance if large sections of the rest of the nation had not been dissatisfied with the new régime. When Napoleon returned to France in the spring of 1815 it was the support of the peasants and artisans which bore him in triumph to Paris.

The difficulties which lay in the path of the Emperor's adjustment to his changed way of life might have been enough in themselves to cause him to return to France when he knew that he could count on popular support, but Louis XVIII and his allies gave him still stronger motives for attempting a *coup d'état*. The revenues of Elba did not meet the cost of his absurd if modest court, and the French government failed to pay any of the annual allowance of 2,000,000 francs it had promised; half the 3,800,000

* Like the Kaiser, Louis XVIII had been forgotten by the mass of the population. It was almost as if France and England had succeeded in restoring the Hohenzollerns in 1939.

† There were 25 francs to the pound sterling in 1815.

francs the Emperor had brought with him were spent by March 1815. More serious still were the rumours of assassination which reached him, and the fact that at Vienna Castlereagh and Talleyrand were discussing exile to a more distant island in the middle of the ocean, such as Santa Lucia. Napoleon expected Marie-Louise and the Prince Imperial to share his retirement, but the Austrian government kept them away.

The decision to return to France was the Emperor's own, and, although he probably considered the project for some months before March 1815, he told no one, and made no preparations until the middle of February, less than a fortnight before his departure. The absence of Campbell, the English commissioner, who left the island on the 10th of February for a holiday which was expected to last for ten or twelve days, gave Napoleon the opportunity to conceal his escape. The first, veiled orders for embarkation were given on the 16th, when Napoleon gave instructions that the brig was to be made ready for a long voyage by the 25th. As the time grew closer, the Emperor's intentions could be no longer concealed, and it was in the presence of a considerable crowd of islanders that he made his way to the harbour and boarded the flagship of his tiny fleet. A little after midnight on the 26th he and his 1,100 men put out to sea.

The troops were disembarked on the 1st of March, after a voyage in which they had come close to discovery. The Emperor had not brought his small Elban army to fight against the much larger forces he could expect to encounter, but to impress the local authorities in the south of France. He gave strict instructions that his followers were not to fire a shot, and the journey to Paris was accomplished entirely without bloodshed. At one stroke he had made the task of opposing him almost impossible. Had they been first attacked his former troops might conceivably have fired upon him, but their unwilling loyalty to Louis XVIII vanished in an instant when they caught sight of the Emperor advancing towards them, supremely confident that they would come to his side, while his own men marched behind him, their arms reversed. Napoleon chose a difficult route which would take him to the Dauphiné, where the population was far more disposed to support him. In Eastern Provence he found scarcely a handful of supporters, but farther inland, where opposition to the repressive measures of the Restoration government was strong, his passage was marked by a mounting wave of enthusiasm amongst the lower classes, who saw him as the incarnation of the Revolution and guarantor of their rights. This rôle was by no means one the Emperor would have chosen for himself, but it lent him widespread popularity, and he was obliged to make concessions to the grievances of the crowds who cheered him with shouts of: "Down with the priests! Down with the nobles! Death to the Royalists! Bourbons to the scaffold!"

When the first confused reports of the landing were received in Marseilles it was merely thought that some of the Elban garrison had tired of life on the island. Elsewhere along the coast there were rumours that the Algerian pirates had made a foray. Communications were primitive, and not until noon on the 5th of March did the news that the Emperor himself had returned to France reach the Ministry of War in Paris. The report had travelled by courier to Lyons and thence by the semaphore telegraph system which linked Lyons with Paris. At first royalist circles in the capital were inclined to treat the affair very lightly; some even believed that it offered an excellent opportunity to dispose of Napoleon once and for all. They were soon undeceived; nothing withstood the usurper. At Grenoble, which he reached after a march of 200 miles in six days, the peasants battered down the gates while the garrison stood by with loaded muskets. The crowd stormed in through the breach and the defenders rushed forward to embrace the Emperor's troops as their general made his escape to the north. If one soldier had been prepared to obey his orders to shoot, the rest might have followed him, but not one of the officers who gave orders to fire on Napoleon's men dared to shoot the first round himself. The size and warmth of the Emperor's welcome at Grenoble assured him of his ultimate success. "Before Grenoble", he would say at St. Helena, "I was an adventurer. At Grenoble I was a reigning prince." The rank and file of the army were delighted by Napoleon's return, but they were not responsible for his restoration as many royalist writers attempted to claim. Despite their own sympathies, and the feelings of their troops, a very large proportion of the officers were scrupulously loyal to Louis XVIII. They did their duty as long as they could and either fled their posts or went over to the Emperor only when it was clear that their men had no intention of resisting him. The troops themselves were swayed far more by the strength of civilian feeling around them than by their own wishes; they were too accustomed to obedience to play the subversive rôle ascribed to them.

Indignant against Napoleon, and promising the King to bring him back to Paris in an iron cage, Ney set off to take command of the 30,000 men concentrated at Lons-le-Saulnier to halt the invasion. He arrived to find the troops disaffected, but for a while he was convinced that they would see the issue in the same light as he did, and would follow him to victory against the Emperor's forces, although they now outnumbered his own. He soon became a prey to doubt. He read the Emperor's proclamation to the army and regretted that soldiers were no longer addressed in such terms. He was beset by bonapartists, and the men in his divisions grew hourly more restive. Napoleon sent him a message, saying that he would shortly greet Ney as he had greeted him the day after the battle of the Moscowa. Yielding to the pressure put upon him from all sides, Ney summoned his troops and announced that he would take them over to the Emperor. At his trial he told the court that he was fearful of provoking civil war. "Could I hold back the sea with my hands?" he asked. "I was caught in the whirlwind and lost my head." The execution of Ney and the other officers who failed to wait a few more days until Louis XVIII, then safe in Belgium, dissolved his army and absolved them from their oaths of loyalty, was the least justifiable act of the second Restoration. The situation in the last days before the King's flight imposed an impossible strain on straightforwardly honest men; the calculating survived. "From the moment of that proclamation" (at Lons-le-Saulnier), said Ney, "I only longed for death. Many a time I have thought of blowing my brains out."

The Marshal met Napoleon at Auxerre, presenting him with a document which attempted to justify his desertion of Louis XVIII. "If you continue to govern tyrannically", it began, "then I am your prisoner rather than your supporter." His manifesto had a kind of consistency with the motives which led Ney to urge the Emperor to abdicate at Fontainebleau in May 1814. "From now onwards the Emperor must govern with one object only, the happiness of the French people and the undoing of the evil which his ambition has brought upon the country." Napoleon received this outburst with a smile, and immediately passed on to practical matters.

None of the government's measures had any effect. After Ney's desertion a notice was found on the railings surrounding the column in the Place Vendôme, which read: "From Napoleon to Louis XVIII, 'My good brother, there is no need to send any more troops, I have enough.'" Louis discussed various proposals for a last defence of his throne. Some of them had at least the merit of originality, particularly the suggestion that the King and his supporters should shut themselves up in the Tuileries and resist all attempts to expel them, thus forcing Napoleon to become the embarrassed author of either a farce or a tragedy. One of the King's more inane advisers urged him to ride in state to meet the usurper outside Paris, where the upstart would be overawed by the living principle of legitimacy, and compelled to beat an ignominious retreat. A little before midnight, while Napoleon slept at Fontaine-bleau, Louis said farewell to his supporters and climbed heavily into his coach to drive to Lille, which was royalist in sympathy and very close to the border. During the night his ministers followed him into exile.

At two o'clock the next afternoon the Emperor left Fontaine-bleau, where his brief visit had not passed without an inspection of the extensive buildings of the palace. As he journeyed towards the capital, the former members and servants of the Imperial Court converged on the Tuileries to take up their old quarters and to prepare to receive their master. "At nine o'clock", writes Houssaye

"a travelling carriage drove rapidly through the gate. It was surrounded by a throng of horsemen of all arms and all ranks, a confused mass waving their swords and roaring, 'Vive l'Empereur!' The half-pay officers filling the courtyard and the generals waiting on the steps of the porch drew their swords and rushed forward. So dense was the crowd, so eager the rush that the horsemen were driven backwards and the postilions came to a halt 10 yards from the Pavillon de Flore. The carriage door was flung open. Napoleon! The crowd seized him, dragged him from his carriage and passed him from hand to hand into

2   *Napoleon Bonaparte*
From the portrait by Robert Lefèvre

3　*Louis XVIII*

From the portrait by Baron Gérard

the entrance hall, where other officers bore him from them, hoisted him shoulder high and carried him to the staircase. . . . . From above the crowd was pouring down the staircase, from below the tide was driving upward. . . . 'For God's sake!' shouted Caulaincourt to Lavallette, 'get in front of him.' Lavallette flung himself forward, turned his back to the crowd, and clinging to the stair-rail made a buttress of his body. Thus he pushed his way backwards up the staircase, step by step, a pace ahead of the Emperor, murmuring all the time, 'It's you, it's you.' And he—he seemed to see nothing, to hear nothing. He was borne forward, his arms extended, his eyes closed, a fixed smile on his face, like a sleepwalker's."

On the 13th of March the powers at Vienna issued a manifesto which declared that as Napoleon had broken the convention which established him as independent sovereign of Elba, he had forfeited all claim to political existence, and was henceforth to be considered beyond the pale of the law. Less than a fortnight later, England, Prussia, Austria and Russia pledged themselves to maintain 150,000 men in the field until Bonaparte had been overthrown. The alliance was cemented by an English subsidy of £5,000,000, to be shared equally amongst her three allies. She also paid indemnities of over £2,000,000, for sending fewer than her quota of men on campaign. A divergence of war aims occurred between Castlereagh and the allied foreign ministers. The three Continental powers were going to war to restore the principle of legitimacy, but in England a significant number of people outside Parliament and a small but vocal section of the Opposition objected to the forthcoming conflict on the grounds that the Bourbons had been too easily expelled to justify their reinstatement. Castlereagh was forced to declare that English war aims were confined to the overthrow of Napoleon and to issue a démenti absolving England from any obligation to restore Louis XVIII. The government received a majority in the House of Commons. As all that had been done was to draw a blank cheque for future action, not necessarily excluding the restoration of Louis XVIII, to Continental minds the whole episode seemed yet another proof of the hypocrisy of the English government, or of the Opposition, or both.

From the moment of his arrival the Emperor was in little doubt that he would have to go to war if he wished to remain on the throne. Within a week of the treaty of alliance on the 25th of March, the allies produced a simple but comprehensive plan to crush Napoleon's army. Three armies, the Austrian, 344,000 men under Schwartzenburg, the English and Prussian, 250,000 under Wellington and Blücher, and the Russian, 200,000 under the ultimate and woolly direction of Alexander I, in all 794,000 troops, would march by converging routes on Paris. A year of peace and a variety of existing commitments had left the allied forces unprepared for an immediate offensive, and until they had concentrated on the French frontier, the Emperor had a breathing space in which to prepare as best he could to defend himself. The situation was desperate, for the royal government had left him an army of 160,000 men capable of active campaigning, and of these a large number would have to remain in garrison along the frontiers when hostilities began. Moreover, Napoleon was still attempting to negotiate for peace with the allied powers, and until he had received a definite refusal, he dared not order mobilisation. The internal political situation presented a number of unfamiliar difficulties. A call to arms would be extremely inadvisable before the last centres of royalist resistance capitulated to the new régime, which happened only on the 16th of April. In view of the slowness of communications—the news of the Emperor's landing in Provence had taken five days to reach the capital—twenty-five days was a short time in which to reassert imperial authority over the whole of the provincial administration, but in 1815 the delay was one he could ill afford.

Napoleon did the best he could while he waited to discover the allies' intentions. Within a week of his arrival in Paris he ordered the establishment of a number of workshops to manufacture and repair the muskets so urgently needed for the mobilisation of a new army. Two days later he instructed Davout, the Minister of War, to begin purchasing remounts for the cavalry. On the 4th of April the Emperor sent personal letters to the four sovereigns of the Alliance protesting the peacefulness of his intentions. Caulaincourt, the Minister of Foreign Affairs, received Castlereagh's answer on the 8th, returning the message to the Prince Regent unopened. The next day saw the publication of the decrees prepared some days before, instructing all undischarged soldiers and the troops who had deserted in April 1814 rather than serve under the Bourbons to return to the army. Response to the decrees varied from one department to another. In Tarn-et-Garonne less than a hundred reported for duty out of more than a thousand whose names appeared on the rolls as liable for service. In the Bouches-du-Rhône only 137 out of 3,283 returned to the colours by the 9th of June, a week before the campaign began. The state of public opinion in some of the western departments did not allow the prefects even to begin the task of mustering the reservists. Nevertheless, the decrees brought in 75,000 men, 17,000 more than the Ministry of War had hoped for. At the same time, the National Guard was mobilised, and although there was no longer any question of being able to transform these approximate equivalents of the Home Guard into regiments of the line, as had been done in the early months of 1814, their presence in fortresses and frontier posts enabled regular soldiers to join the striking force now being grouped in the most immediately dangerous area, the north-east frontier.

Against the vast forces about to march on France, the Emperor had the army he inherited from Louis XVIII, the deserters and reservists who had obeyed the decrees of the 9th of April, and 15,000 volunteers. The problem of creating an adequate army would have been comparatively simple had the Emperor been able to call up the hundreds of thousands of his old conscripts, but the most popular act of his predecessor's short reign had been to abolish all forms of conscription, and Napoleon did not dare to prejudice his return to power by mobilising men whose sole desire was to remain civilian. The Emperor had left France prostrate, but by the time he came back, the freedom of the press conceded by Louis XVIII, and the political activity caused by the Restoration and the flight of the King, had made the French far less manageable than they had been under ten years of autocracy. Napoleon was obliged to guarantee the liberties accorded by the Bourbons, and summon the Chambers as the price of his restoration to the throne; it was a disagreeable experience and one which put unfamiliar obstacles in the path of raising an army quickly.

Sailors were withdrawn from a fleet made useless by English naval supremacy, and turned into soldiers, of a sort; six foreign regiments were raised; every legal expedient to find troops was

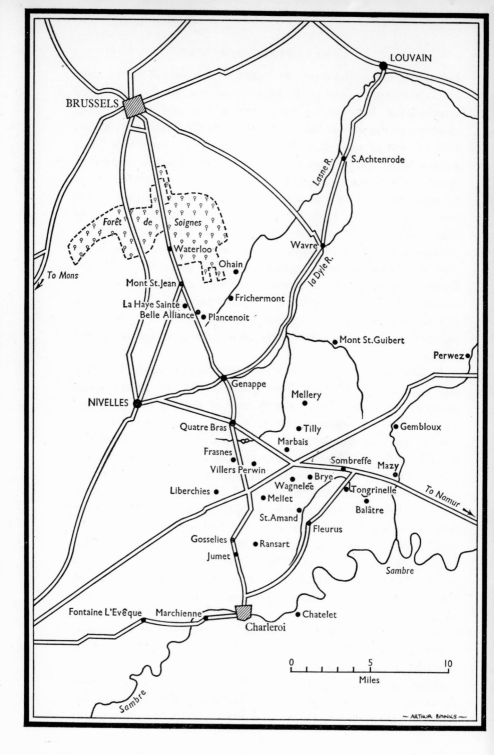

The Campaign of 1815

employed. Napoleon repeatedly turned his thoughts to the conscription class of 1815. These men had been *appelé en activité* eighteen months before, in October 1813, at a last scraping of the barrel to make good the losses of the Russian Campaign; most of them were then too young to serve, but by the 1st of March, 1814, 80,000 had gone to the depots where they spent the last weeks of the war undergoing some military training. Altogether the class of 1815 numbered 120,000 men, and their presence in the army would have solved the most pressing man-power problems. The Emperor was anxious to mobilise them, and believed that the country would tolerate this modest incursion into conscription. Davout opposed the scheme, refusing to issue such an order, and when Napoleon laid the proposal before the Conseil d'État on the 23rd of May, they adopted a similar attitude, adding disingenuously that they did not feel competent to exercise powers which were the prerogative of the Chambers. A week later the Emperor hit on the idea of treating the class of 1815 as undischarged soldiers, and therefore legally obliged to report for service. By the 11th of June 46,000 were en route for the depots, without any significant opposition being shown to their departure, for the country had at last resigned itself to a continuation of the war with Europe; but the shift in public opinion had come too late to save Napoleon, and the campaign was lost before any of the class of 1815 had reached the army.

Prodigious efforts were required to equip the army in time to take the offensive by the middle of 1815, and its appearance in Belgium on the 15th of June was a tribute to the energy which the Emperor could infuse into his administrators, and to the skill and loyalty of the officials in the Ministry of War. Thousands of horses had to be found for the cavalry and artillery. The clothing stores had been run down in 1813 and 1814, and the Restoration government, short of money and pacifically disposed, had allowed the stocks to sink to vanishing point. By the end of May the output of the Parisian workshops had reached 1,250 uniforms per day. At Vincennes 12,000,000 cartridges were made in two months, while by early June the daily production of new muskets rose to 2,000, and three times that number of reconditioned weapons were despatched to the depots.

The Emperor had made the best use he could of the time that was given him; in eight weeks the strength of the army had been increased by 80,000 men, and the numbers joining the ranks would continue to mount until by autumn there would be well over half a million men under arms. Napoleon's strategy was determined by the preparedness of the allies, and as early as the 27th of April he had decided to make his main effort in the north-east, where he planned to strike a crushing blow against Blücher and Wellington before the Austrians and Russians were ready to take the offensive along the Rhine. In May a revolt in the Vendée obliged him to send 13,000 troops to police the area, and in addition to them he had to leave thousands in the depots, and *corps d'observation* to cover the frontier when he sent out orders for the concentration of the Army of the North. Nevertheless, when the forces for the invasion gathered around Beaumont he had succeeded in assembling 124,000 fully-armed, fully-equipped men.

Wellington reached Brussels to take up his command on the 5th of April. His army numbered 24,200, English, Dutch, Belgians, Brunswickers and Hanoverians, and the majority of his 4,000 English and 7,000 Hanoverians were recruits. The loyalty of most of the 2,000 Belgians was extremely doubtful, for only a year before they had been serving under Napoleon. Next day the Duke wrote a despondent letter to Lord Bathurst:

> " . . . It appears to me that you have not taken in England a clear view of your situation, that you do not think war certain, and that a great effort must be made, if it is hoped that it shall be short. You have not called out the militia, or announced such an intention in your message to Parliament, by which measure your troops of the line in Ireland and elsewhere might become disposable. . . . If you could let me have 40,000 good British infantry, besides those you insist on having in garrisons, the proportion settled by treaty that you are to furnish of cavalry . . . and 150 pieces of British field artillery fully horsed, I should be satisfied, and take my chance with the rest, and engage that we would play our part in the game. But, as it is, we are in a bad way."

The build-up of Wellington and Blücher's armies throughout April and May did not bring the Duke much confidence; Napoleon was lessening his disadvantage with every week that passed. By June, Blücher's four corps, based on Charleroi, Namur, Ciney and

Liége, had grown to 120,000. On the day before the campaign began Wellington's strength was 93,717, but of these only 31,253 were British—most of them had never seen a shot fired in anger— and 29,214 were Dutch-Belgians. The remainder of this polyglot force was composed of the King's German Legion, Hanoverians and Brunswickers, of whom only the German Legion, old Peninsular veterans, could be relied on in a crisis. The Duke had every reason to be gloomy: "I have an infamous army," he wrote to Lord Stewart, his Adjutant-General in Spain, "very weak and ill-equipped, and a very inexperienced staff." Yet, with the exception of the Dutch-Belgians, these troops were to surpass all expectations in the days that followed.

2

The Arms

WITHOUT SOME KNOWLEDGE of the weapons with which Wellington's men fought the battle of Waterloo, a detailed account of the campaign of 1815 loses much of its interest. The musket with which three-quarters of the English army were armed seems at first sight to belong to an almost mythical past, and the tactics to which it gave rise quite absurdly heroic; yet the tactics of the early nineteenth century were anything but unscientific, and represented the best use to which the arms of the period could be put.

The English musket, the Brown Bess, was in essence a smooth-bored, muzzle-loading, late seventeenth-century flintlock, to which the passage of a century and a half had brought only a few minor improvements. In the hands of well-trained troops it might be fired as often as twice a minute, but such a rate could not be kept up for long. The cartridges were made by hand, usually by women, the cases consisting of strong paper, hence the modern stationer's term, cartridge paper, and were well waxed to preserve them against damp. Using them was a complicated operation. The cartridge had to be cut with a knife or torn open with the teeth, and a small amount of powder sprinkled in the firing pan; the rest of the explosive was poured down the muzzle, with the ball and a small wad, and rammed tight with a ramrod.* The charge was fired by a spark from the flint igniting the powder in the priming pan which in turn detonated the explosive in the barrel.

Gunpowder, a mixture of charcoal, sulphur and saltpetre, had first appeared on the battlefield in the early fourteenth century, but

---

* Inexperienced soldiers, overcome by the novelty of being under fire for the first time, often forgot to remove their ramrods before pressing the trigger. Unless they could pick up another, their muskets became virtually useless.

for the next 500 years no substantial advance was made on this rather unsatisfactory propellant. When a musket was fired, half the powder remained as a deposit fouling the barrel or left the muzzle in a cloud of dense white smoke. Until smokeless powder was introduced in the 1880's, battles were fought in very poor visibility, and it was common for troops to fire on their own side, and for generals to mistake what was happening in the enemy lines, as a number did at Waterloo.* The flint which ignited the powder in the priming pan had to be changed after every thirty shots, and when the pan became foul from the priming, which it frequently did, the flint missed fire. Ramming became more difficult after the first few shots because of the deposits accumulating on the side of the barrel, and if it was dispensed with, the escape of gases was so great that the ball lost most of its force. "When hard pressed", wrote Sergeant-Major Cotton of the 7th Hussars, "the infantry would resort to the French skirmishers' method of loading in order to save time. After priming, they would shake the rest of the powder into the barrel, dropping the ball after it, and then giving the butt a rap or two on the ground, which was quite soft after so much rain. The ball, in consequence, not being rammed down to confine the powder, came out at times quite harmless." Yet however cumbersome and inefficient a weapon the English musket may seem, the French pattern was inferior. Its greatest short-coming was that it was used with coarser powder, so that although English shot was a quarter as heavy again, and therefore required a heavier charge, the French barrel needed washing out twice as often, after every fifty shots instead of every hundred. Rifles made their appearance some time before Waterloo, but without a breech-loading mechanism to accompany the rifling, they were not really suitable for military purposes. The Rifle Brigade, who took part in the Waterloo Campaign, were equipped with Baker's rifle, which was much more accurate than the musket, and had a longer range, but could only be fired a third as often, so great was the difficulty of ramming a charge down a rifled barrel.

A musket ball could inflict mortal injury at a distance of as much

* "The smoke hung so thick about [at Waterloo] that, although not more than 80 yards asunder, we could only distinguish each other by the flashes of the pieces."

as 500 yards, but the weapon was so inaccurate that at this range a hit was completely accidental; at 250 yards the French musket was subject to an error of 9 feet. Troops usually held their fire until the enemy were within 100 yards of them, and the returns of a practice company of ordinary German soldiers of the period explain why this was so. The Germans ranked above the French and below the English in accuracy of fire, and their performance, although without the distraction of battlefield conditions, may be taken as giving a reasonable picture of the value of musket fire. Firing at a target 100 feet long and 6 feet high, that is to say at the kind of target a company of infantry would offer in action, 60% of their shots hit the screen at 75 yards. At double this distance only 40% of their rounds were successful, and at 225 yards only one ball in four found the target.

With the help of such facts the tactics of the Napoleonic Wars begin to make sense. The infantryman was compelled to fire from the shoulder in an awkward and vulnerable standing position because he could only load standing up. He waited to fire until he was almost upon the enemy because his musket was inaccurate, and because an appreciable time would have to elapse before he could fire again. The troops were drawn up almost shoulder to shoulder, and often in more than one rank in order to achieve a reasonable concentration of fire-power. Because the enemy was no better armed, the massed infantry formations of Wellington's army were not as dangerous as they seemed. The deployment and evolutions of the early nineteenth-century army may still be studied on the modern parade-ground, where they have survived virtually unchanged. In those days parades had more than a ceremonial and vaguely disciplinary value; they provided a daily opportunity to rehearse the movements the soldiers would perform under fire. The pompous occasions which are now retained out of feeling for tradition were then largely practical affairs. Colours were trooped because the regiment fought closely grouped around its standard, which provided a convenient rallying point for stragglers gone astray in the smoke clouds surrounding their position, as well as being a focus of morale for troops compelled to stand their ground for long periods while the issue of the struggle was slowly, but nonetheless, bloodily, decided.

At Waterloo the English possessed a considerable advantage in fire-power over their opponents. Their superiority was of long standing, and possibly dated from the Middle Ages, when the English archers were renowned for their accuracy. This, like their reputation for steadiness in defence, probably owed as much to national character as did the French gift for swift manœuvre and dash in the attack. Until a few years before Waterloo the English army, like the French, had arranged infantry in three ranks, the theory being that by the time the third rank had fired its volley, the first would have reloaded. It was noticed that the presence of the third rank tended to hinder the firing and reloading of the other two, and that given the well-trained soldiers of the English army, reducing the number of ranks to two did not diminish the rate of fire; moreover dispensing with the third rank increased the line, and therefore the regiment's fire-power, by 50%. Among the pioneers of the two-rank system was Sir John Moore, who fell at Corunna, and Wellington, his successor in the Peninsula, reaped the fruits of his innovations in Belgium as well as Spain. The English development of scientific infantry tactics was fostered by the possession of a small standing army, in contrast to the vast conscript force recruited by France to maintain the conquests of the Revolution and Empire. Nevertheless, it is surprising that after a brief experiment with two ranks the French should have returned to three, still not realising that fire-power was the decisive factor in infantry engagements.

A striking contrast existed between the infantry tactics of the two armies; since the Revolution the French had favoured an assault in column while the English perfected the traditional defence in line. The columnar attack drew most of its strength from the moral effect a mass of troops would have on the thin, extended line of defenders, and this system sufficed to win resounding victories against a number of European armies. It ignored the fact that if the defenders stopped to fire at the advancing column, the issue would be settled not by appearances but by musket fire, because for all its clumsiness, the weapon was lethal at short range. Although the defenders in line could all fire at once, only the two front rows of the column were able to reply. If the column attempted to deploy in line to meet fire with fire, the loss of time and the confusion which resulted merely brought further casualties at a very small price to the enemy. In the Peninsula the English became so systematic in exploiting the weaknesses of the attack in column that they would wait until the column had almost gained their positions, close in from either flank until the French were surrounded on three sides, and then fire their first volley. Most of the men in the column were as helpless as if they had marched up empty-handed, and within thirty seconds the English had reloaded and were ready to fire again, while the enemy were still struggling to free themselves of their dead and wounded. At times Wellington's regiments enjoyed fire superiority of ten to one over columns their own size, but their success was dependent of the use of seasoned, properly trained troops.

Under ideal conditions, every infantry assault was made and received with the support of the two other arms of the contemporary army, the cavalry and artillery. Ideal conditions rarely obtained, and a commander needed considerable skill to overcome the difficulties which hindered the combined use of all three arms. He had in the first place no better way of communicating with the formations taking part in an attack than the primitive means of sending a messenger who might be wounded or even lose his way in the confusion through which he had to travel. Furthermore, a good deal of the field might be invisible because of the clouds of smoke which, on a windless day, might hang over the scene of the actual fighting for several hours, making it hard to see whether or not orders were being carried out. Finally, the commander had to solve the problem of making sure that the cavalry and artillery made their contributions at the decisive moment.

The typical attack was preceded by a cannonade from the foot artillery, guns massed to lay down heavy barrages and which rarely moved during the engagement. As the cannonade died down the infantry moved forward in column, accompanied by horse batteries which shelled the troops blocking the immediate line of advance. Expertly handled, the completely mobile horse batteries could greatly ease the infantry's task. They were trained to fire quickly, relimber, overtake the marching column once more, and fire again at the enemy infantry and artillery, dispersing the defender's lines and replying to the guns which were firing grape-shot into the attackers.

In front of the massed infantry there was usually a screen of skirmishers, or sharpshooters, whose job it was to harass the defenders with irregular fire at fairly close range, a move the enemy countered by sending out a similar force to hold them off. Should the attack succeed in shaking the defending troops, but not be strong enough to dislodge them from their positions, a cavalry charge was often all that was needed to scatter their line, provided that they were not given time to form squares. Within a few minutes of a successful cavalry charge, formations dissolved, a breach was opened in the front, through which the cavalry poured, followed by the infantry. Closely pursued, the retreating enemy infantrymen would not be given the opportunity to regroup, and the battle would be over.

Battles were rarely, if ever, so easily won. The cavalry, shock-weapon though they were, were vulnerable to a number of counter-measures. Should the defenders bring up their own cavalry in an organised charge, the isolated horsemen mopping up infantry resistance and spreading panic up and down the rear were caught at a hopeless disadvantage. Cavalry could also be driven off by steady artillery fire, and infantry squares were still more effective in exposing the cavalry charge as a sharp but very brittle weapon. The horseman had no answer to a wall of bayonets, and a succession of crashing volleys of musket fire. His sabre, or his lance, if he carried one, were hardly effective against a number of bayonets, and he found it hard to fire his carbine or pistol accurately, and harder still to load them again. A body of cavalry could ride down a scattered infantry or a group of gunners with horrifying ease, but if thrown against squares of infantry undistracted by enemy musket fire, and if, as at Waterloo, the squares were supported by artillery, there was only one outcome to an unaccompanied cavalry attack, the rapid destruction of the most expensive and most precious troops in the army.

Cavalry were indispensable to the effective waging of Napoleonic war; their superior mobility and speed made them the advance and rear guards of an army tied to the marching pace of the infantry. On the eve of Waterloo we find the Emperor attempting to catch up with the English retreating from Quatre Bras and bring them to battle by sending forward all the cavalry he can collect, while

Wellington is able to give his infantry time to escape by leaving behind his cavalry and horse artillery to delay the French squadrons. In open campaign the cavalry provided a screen which advanced in front of the army, establishing routes, protecting defiles, and sending back a series of reports to the marching columns of infantry. The most spectacular use of cavalry followed a decisive battle, for they conducted the pursuit which justified the loss of life and material on the battlefield. As they overtook the retreating army they forced it to turn and fight at a disadvantage, or else scatter in panic out of their path in an irredeemable rout in which the dispersal of men and the loss of cannon and supplies made it impossible to bring the army together again. In the Peninsula the lack of enough good cavalry frequently robbed Wellington of the fruits he had earned in successful battles, and the number and excellence of Napoleon's cavalry indicate the importance he placed on a corps whose training and equipment were the most costly and troublesome of all.

Wellington had fewer guns at Waterloo than his opponent, but the French artillery were inferior in quality to the English, and their superior numbers did not bring them much advantage. Some of the credit for their failure must go to the Duke, who followed his invariable practice of placing as many of his infantry as possible out of reach of the French guns. Such a precaution might seem an obvious one, yet it made Wellington's battles remarkable amongst those of his period, so accustomed were commanders to draw up their armies within view of the enemy. The English were incomparably better off than the French in their mobile field batteries. Horse artillery, as opposed to foot artillery, where the gunners marched by the side of the gun carriages, which remained stationary in action, had only been properly introduced after the beginning of the Revolution.

Of all the European armies the English had been most successful in exploiting this new development; their training and equipment were far superior to anything the French had ever seen. The new field artillery, whose inspiration had been French, was composed of six-gun batteries; Captain Mercer's had nine-pounders, which had been made as self-sufficient and mobile as possible by mounting all the numerous personnel on horses or carriages. Mercer's six guns required an establishment of five officers, a surgeon, 187 N.C.O.s and men, one farrier, two collar makers and a wheeler, and 226 horses. The ability of horse batteries to move quickly about the field multiplied Wellington's strength in guns at threatened points along the front. So great was the impression made by the outnumbered English batteries at Waterloo that the French Ministry of War set up a committee of artillery officers to report on the allied artillery detachments taking part in a grand review held in October 1818. The English were easily the best, they concluded, adding that no French battery could have cleared the ground so well. "By mounting the gunners on the gun-limbers and waggon, by ridding them of their cumbrous and useless carbines, and by attaching the knapsacks to the carriages . . . the English have made the Field Batteries a new arm."

There was little difference between the performance of French and English guns. The rate of fire was about that of the musket, that is to say, with skill and exertion, the guns could be fired twice a minute. No means had been found to overcome recoil action, and the pieces had to be laid afresh after every round. The extreme range of a twelve-pounder, the largest gun commonly used in battle, was about 3,600 yards, but the extreme effective range was 1,200 yards to 1,700 yards. It was only at little more than half this distance, however, that firing usually began. A variety of shot was used, ball, canister and grape. The last two spread their contents over a wide area; at short range they were extremely effective against infantry and cavalry in close formations. Canister represented a crude form of machine-gun fire in that it contained ordinary musket balls, while grape composed of small iron scrap might be thought of as an equally remote forerunner of shrapnel. To achieve any kind of range, it was necessary to fall back on single balls, which inflicted serious casualties on columns of infantry, where they would knock several men down at once, remaining dangerous as long as they continued to travel. Ensign Leeke, of the 52nd Regiment, had the not unusual but terrifying experience of watching a cannon-ball leave the gun and travel towards him:

> "After we had been stationed for an hour or so far down in front of the British position, a gleam of sunshine, falling on them, particularly attracted my attention to some brass guns

in our front which appeared to be placed lower down the French slope, and nearer to us, than the others; I distinctly saw the French artilleryman go through the whole process of spunging out one of the guns and reloading it; I could see that it was pointed at our square, and when it was discharged I caught sight of the ball, which appeared to be in a direct line for me. I thought, Shall I move? No! I gathered myself up, and stood firm, with the colour in my right hand. I do not exactly know the rapidity with which cannon-balls fly, but I think that two seconds elapsed from the time I saw this shot leave the gun until it struck the front face of the square. It did not strike the four men in rear of whom I was standing, but the four poor fellows on their right. It was fired at some elevation, and struck the front man about the knees, and coming to the ground under the feet of the rear man of the four, whom it most severely wounded, it rose, and passing within an inch or two of the colour poles, went over the rear face of the square without doing any further injury. The two men in the first and second ranks fell outward, I fear they did not survive long; the two others fell within the square. The rear man made a considerable outcry on being wounded, but on one of the officers saying kindly to him, 'O man, don't make a noise', he instantly recollected himself and was quiet.... I should not omit to mention that it was said, after the action, that a round shot had expended its force on the solid square of the 71st Highland L.I. on our right front, and only stopped when it had killed or wounded seventeen men; I can easily suppose this to be possible from what I saw of the effects of the shot which passed so close to me."

The strangest artillery unit to take the field at Waterloo, and in the light of modern developments, the most interesting, was Whinyates' rocket troop. The rockets used were those invented a few years before by Sir William Congreve, and had a maximum range of 3,500 yards. These missiles were too unreliable to be of much value, and it is surprising that the British army continued to send them on active service. Whinyates was an enthusiast, but Wellington was not.

"Captain Whinyates", writes Mercer, "having joined the army with the rocket troop, the Duke, who looked upon rockets as nonsense, ordered that they should be put into store, and the troops supplied with guns instead. Colonel Sir G. Wood, instigated by Whinyates, called on the Duke to ask his permission to leave him his rockets as well as his guns. A refusal. Sir George, however, seeing that the Duke was in a particular good humour, ventured to say, 'It will break poor Whinyates'

heart to lose his rockets.' 'Damn his heart, Sir; let my order
be obeyed', was the answer thundered forth by the Duke, as
he turned on the worthy Sir George."

Nevertheless, the Duke relented, on condition that the rocketeers took guns with them, and Mercer met Whinyates using his
rockets on the retreat from Quatre Bras to Waterloo.

"Meanwhile the rocketeers had placed a little iron triangle on
the road with a rocket lying on it. The order to fire is given—
portfire applied—the fidgety missile begins to sputter out
sparks and wriggle its tail for a second or so, and then darts
forth straight up the chaussée. A gun stands right in its way,
between which the shell in the head of the rocket bursts, the
gunners fall left and right, and, those of the other guns taking
to their heels, the battery is deserted in an instant. Strange;
but so it was, I saw them run, and for some minutes afterwards
I saw the guns standing mute and unmanned, whilst our
rocketeers kept shooting off rockets, none of which ever
followed the course of the first; most of them, on arriving
about the middle of the ascent, took a vertical direction, whilst
some actually turned back on ourselves—and one of these,
following me like a squib until its shell exploded, actually put
me in more danger than all the fire of the enemy throughout
that day. Meanwhile, the French artillerymen, seeing how the
land lay, returned to their guns and opened a fire of case-shot
on us, but without effect, for we retreated to our ridge without
the loss of a man, or even any wounded, though the range
could not have been above 200 yards."

English tactical superiority almost certainly turned the scales at
Waterloo. Wellington had slightly fewer men in the field until
late in the day, many of them were poor material—some of the
foreign regiments deserted their posts during the battle—and the
Emperor should have overwhelmed them long before the Prussians
arrived on the scene. The Imperial army, the finest Napoleon had
assembled since the days of Austerlitz, was composed very largely
of veterans whose enthusiasm was at fever pitch. With the exception
of a limited number of good regiments, Wellington's patchwork
force and Blücher's conscripts were man for man no match for the
French. The Emperor's defeat astonished Europe as well as himself,
and to the present day, explanations have usually been sought in
every direction save the right one, the technical skill of the English
army.

The Emperor had spent no more than a short time in Spain

early on in the Peninsular Campaigns, and had scarcely seen the English army for himself. Like most people he was convinced that his armies had been defeated in Spain partly because he himself had not been there, and partly because the conditions had been unusually difficult: he could point to the appalling communications and the savage guerrilla warfare which had so often hamstrung French operations. He was certainly not disposed to listen to the officers who had had long experience of the English. On the morning of Waterloo he pooh-poohed Soult and Reille when they warned him that his arrangements might not be adequate to the task of defeating the English. Given Napoleon's temperament, to say nothing of his preoccupation as head of state, it is not very surprising that he should have remained so incredulous of the virtues of the English army. They were technical, tactical virtues, and the Emperor had never bothered greatly about tactics. A remarkably small number of innovations were made during the fifteen years he was absolute master of the French army and state and his throne depended on the superiority of his army. Because he was first of all a politician and only secondly a soldier, his interest in warfare lay in the political results battle might achieve, and in the later years of his career, once he had placed his army in a favourable position to fight a decisive battle, he left the details of the encounter to his subordinates. He had made a half-hearted attempt to reduce the three-rank system to two: "the third rank serves no purpose when firing, and even less in a bayonet charge", he wrote to Marmont in 1813, and although he was clearly quite aware of the advantages of the English system, he was so indifferent to tactical improvements that he suffered the return to three ranks.

At the outset of the revolutionary wars, almost a quarter of a century before, the French army established a superiority over its Continental opponents which it had never lost as long as it was not heavily outnumbered. Complacency was the inevitable result of continual success. Against the background of European war on a vast scale it was easy to ignore the achievements of the tiny English force in the Peninsula. "The English infantry", wrote the future Marshal Bugeaud, who had met it as a young officer in Spain, "is the finest in the world. Fortunately, it is small." His less thoughtful contemporaries grasped only that it was a small army and a professional one. For them the professional army had been discredited in the first years of the revolutionary wars, when the conscripts of the Republic had swept away the cumbersome and ridiculous forces of the *ancien régime*. The new French army employed fresh tactics, taking some from the reformers of the old royal army, and adopting others from sheer necessity: raw soldiers could not be expected to perform the complicated manœuvres practised by professional troops. The reformed French methods proved irresistible against neighbouring armies whose commanders still thought in terms of the wars of the mid-eighteenth century. With the passage of time the haphazard circumstances which had accompanied the early republican victories were turned into a regular system. The ablest of the generals of the Republic, Napoleon Bonaparte, made himself head of state, and harnessing the resources of France to his own ambition, took the new military doctrine to its greatest triumphs. Within a dozen years the streets of Rome, Vienna, Madrid and Moscow echoed to the march of French troops, and very reluctantly, the European powers were obliged to imitate the state which had destroyed their professional armies and the old rules of war at the same time.

At first sight the English army in 1815, the only remaining professional force, was the least reformed in Europe. At Waterloo, however, English techniques overthrew the premises on which the French had built their astonishing successes since the beginning of the revolutionary wars twenty-three years before. The exclusive triumph of English methods is partly explained by the fact that the Continental powers began to reconstruct their armies with the French at their frontiers, and continued the task after their armies had been crushed in successive campaigns. England had led the European alliances against France, but apart from the comparatively small diversion she created in Spain, on land she did little more than provide the cash while her allies provided the cannon-fodder. Protected by her sea-power, England had time to learn the new lessons slowly, to distinguish between substance and reality in current military practice. It is for this reason that the eighteenth-century appearance of the English army was deceptive. To believe, as many contemporaries did, that conscript armies were more efficient than professional was to argue not by reason but by association. The English army was ideally suited to the warfare of the early nineteenth century; the troops were long-service volunteers, well equipped, thoroughly trained and ferociously disciplined. What they lacked in dash they made up for in method and stolidity, and in Wellington they had a general who could make good use of their qualities.

Bugeaud's description of English defensive tactics in the Peninsula throws a great deal of light on the shortcomings of the assault column against steady troops where no attempt was made at a flanking movement. The scene he depicts was typical of the later battles of the Empire, when manœuvre became a rarity in the French army, and the French soldier's greatest talents, mobility and improvisation, were thrown away.

"The English generally occupied well chosen defensive positions having a certain command, and they showed only a portion of their forces. The usual artillery action first took place. Soon, in great haste, without studying the position, without taking time to examine if there were means to make a flank attack, we marched straight on, taking the bull by the horns. About 1,000 yards from the English line the men became excited, spoke to one another and hurried their march; the column began to be a little confused. The English remained quite silent with ordered arms, and from their steadiness appeared to be a long red wall. This steadiness invariably produced an effect on the young soldiers. Very soon we got nearer, shouting *Vive l'Empereur! en avant! à la baionnette!* Shakos were raised on the muzzles of the muskets; the column began to double, the ranks got into confusion, the agitation produced a tumult; shots were fired as we advanced. The English line remained silent, still and immovable, with ordered arms, even when we were only 300 yards distant, and it appeared to ignore the storm about to break. The contrast was striking; in our inmost thoughts each felt that the enemy was a long time in firing, and this fire reserved for so long, would be very unpleasant when it did come. Our ardour cooled. The moral power of steadiness, which nothing shakes (even if it be only appearance), over disorder which stupefies itself with noise, overcame our minds. At this moment of intense excitement, the English wall shouldered arms; an indescribable feeling rooted many of our men to the spot; they began to fire. The enemy's steady concentrated volleys swept our ranks; decimated, we turned round seeking to recover our equilibrium; then three deafening cheers broke the silence of our opponents; at the third they were on us, pushing our disorganised flight."

Like all unsatisfactory military techniques, attack in column had once served a useful purpose; it made the best use of the inexperienced troops of the early Republican armies, who lacked the discipline to maintain linear formations under fire and the refinements of movement which went with them, and it enabled a commander to move large numbers over the battlefield in a compact body. Once the soldiers became seasoned troops, and the column began to be directed in direct attacks against strongly defended positions, its *raison d'être* had largely disappeared. Nevertheless, the innovations hardened into a system whose original purpose was lost in mechanical repetition, and for this Napoleon, as master of the French army, must bear the blame. In his first and most brilliant campaign, in Italy, in 1796, Napoleon was obliged to overcome his numerical inferiority by the use of tactical finesse. Once firmly established in power, and able to levy a vast annual blood tax from France and her satellites, like almost every other commander cursed with ample numbers of men and material, the Emperor came increasingly to rely not on superior tactics but on brute force to win his battles. The battles of the later Empire were bloody, sledge-hammer affairs, in which resource and ingenuity were abandoned for the senseless multiplication of numbers attacking unweakened points. Although Napoleon was able, and willing, to pay an appalling price in lives for his victories, ironically, he drew far less profit from the blood-baths of Friedland, Essling and Borodino than he had gained in Italy when he was obliged to husband his forces and depend on his wits. "I have fought sixty battles", he remarked at the end of his career, "and I have learned nothing that I did not know at the outset." He exaggerated; he had, in fact, come to forget a great deal. Jomini described his later years more accurately when he wrote: "One might say that he was sent into this world to teach generals and statesmen what they ought to avoid."

The Emperor's example seems to have infected his army down to the lowest ranks. The army of Waterloo bore only a superficial resemblance to the superb war machine that had electrified Europe a few years before. Blind courage, dash in the attack, self-intoxication with the idea of *gloire*, had driven out all thought of the worth of accurate musket fire and indirect manœuvre. The veterans' experience of a dozen battlefields and a score of engagements were made to count for little more than steadiness under fire and fruitless heroism in the attack. In an earlier guise their methods had achieved the status of shock tactics, but by 1815, as Wellington and a number of discerning French officers could see, nothing was more obvious than the sterility of the blind assault in columns. The fate of the Imperial Guard at Waterloo serves as epigraph for the empty victories and resounding defeats of the years after 1809; they were marched *en masse* to destruction at the hands of the English infantry deployed in line and supported by the redoubtable horse artillery. It was magnificent, but it was no longer war.

3

The Men

THERE WERE AS MANY CONTRASTS between administration and recruitment in the French and English armies of 1815 as there were between the ways in which they fought, and for much the same reasons, the difference in size and the experience of the Revolution. Just as the tactics of the other Continental forces had been influenced by the developments in France, so had the composition and organisation of their armies, and if the English appeared, by virtue of their security and isolation, to remain in the eighteenth century, in reality they had adopted an alternative convention. The evolution of the English army, like that of the society from which it sprang, can give the misleading impression of an archaic institution unaffected by European experience, when in fact it has merely substituted piecemeal and empiric reconstruction for organic reform.

One of the most striking differences between the two armies was in the recruitment of the officer corps. As a result of universal conscription and the disappearance during the Revolution of most of the noble families which had previously officered the army, most of Napoleon's officers had been promoted from the ranks. They were, on the whole, worse off than their English counterparts, not so much because the English were rather better paid, but because the majority of Wellington's officers possessed some private means.* The army of 1815 was still small enough for the gentry and aristocracy to receive an overwhelming proportion of the King's commissions, and promotion was organised in a way unthinkable in an egalitarian society. There were two methods of

* The English officers' mess was an institution the French could not afford to imitate.

41

advancement in Wellington's army, one by simple purchase, for so much cash, the other by merit and good service. The second method was quite inadequate. At the time of Waterloo the practice was to fill vacancies caused by death or incapacitation in action by promotion inside the regiment without money changing hands, while in all other circumstances promotion was by purchase, with the use of influence where a number of candidates presented themselves for a single post. Officers who lacked the money to pay for advancement progressed slowly if their units failed to come under fire very often. "There might be a lieutenant-colonel of twenty-six", wrote Oman, "who had risen rapidly by purchase or interest, and captains of fifty or even sixty." The most surprising thing about this system is that it led to remarkably little resentment between officers so variously treated; it must have seemed as inevitable as the appointment of wealthy and influential young men to directorships in modern industry or seats in Parliament.

The commissioning of outstanding N.C.O.s to vacancies caused in action occurred more frequently than might be supposed, but as they lacked the funds to purchase routine promotion, it is not surprising that even the ablest officers who came from the ranks should have been fortunate to rise to major; and according to Oman, only one seems to have become a colonel. There was no more outrageous example of the system in Wellington's army than the Commander-in-Chief himself. Despite his early successes in India, until he had established his reputation in the Peninsula, his meteoric career* was due solely to family connections, and it was on these grounds that the Opposition challenged his appointment as Commander-in-Chief in Portugal. Yet just as Wellington disarmed these perfectly well-founded assertions, so, by and large, his subordinates redeemed the utterly irrational manner in which they achieved their commands. In much the same way contemporary English political life succeeded remarkably often in producing able and responsible administrators, despite the absurdity of rotten boroughs and aristocratic connection. The French, who were naturally disposed to be critical of their opponents, thought the English army well officered, and even General Foy, the most

* See Appendix.

discriminating of French observers, who found fault with so many other aspects of the Duke's army, was loud in his praise of its officers.

Formal training for officers, except those in the Artillery and Engineers, was in its extreme infancy, and when a young man joined the army as an ensign, usually at seventeen or eighteen, he had to pick up the rudiments of his profession as best he could. The first months were largely spent in learning drill. For the serious-minded there existed a considerable number of books on war, most of them foreign, and the pamphlets put out by the War Office as guides to the conduct of the more responsible posts to which an officer might be appointed. Captain William Hay received a far less casual grounding than most, for when he joined the 52nd Light Infantry in 1808 the regiment was very much under the influence of Sir John Moore's reforming ideas.

"At the youthful age of sixteen I joined my regiment, the rules of which at that time were most strict and perfect for young officers, having been drawn up by Sir John Moore himself. The sum he stipulated as yearly allowance in addition to pay was not to exceed £100; but £80 he considered sufficient to enable an officer to live as a gentleman, without getting into debt. My father allowed me the larger sum. I, with the other youngsters, was handed over to the Adjutant, Lieutenant Shaw, for drill, it being the rule of the regiment that all young officers must be drilled for six months in the ranks with the men before being allowed to do duty as an officer. These drills consisted of five hours each day, besides morning and evening parades, and we were kept well occupied with our military duties."

Wellington, unlike Napoleon and Blücher, possessed no Chief of Staff, and the work normally supervised by one man was shared amongst three officials. The first of these was a Military Secretary, whose actual importance was small, and whose function, as the title suggests, was to conduct the correspondence between Wellington and his subordinates. The two others, the Adjutant-General and Quartermaster-General between them discharged the administrative duties of a chief of staff. Although by comparison with modern times, the business of running an army was then far less complicated, the movement, quartering and provisioning of 100,000 men involved a considerable amount of staff work even when reduced to their simplest terms, and the Adjutant- and

Quartermaster-Generals were seconded by a considerable number of Assistants and Deputy Assistants.

The rank and file of Wellington's army have retained a shadowy and unsavoury reputation in popular history. The Duke's remarks on the inadequacy of some of the allied troops he commanded in the Waterloo Campaign, "an infamous army", etc., became unfairly attached to the English army of the period, and the changes in English society over the last 150 years have confirmed the widespread belief that the average English infantryman belonged to a crew of criminals, no doubt well fitted for the straightforward warfare of the age, but hardly representative of their civilian contemporaries. There were two good reasons for such an impression: the army was the traditional home for the ne'er-do-well and social misfit, and its members received more publicity than the rural peasantry. The ordinary soldier does not seem very distinguishable from his equals at home, and his behaviour and amusements scarcely varied from theirs. Except on campaign his conditions were little harder, and sometimes a good deal easier, while his pay and allowances made him better off than many farm labourers. A number of Wellington's sergeants have left autobiographies and letters; their accounts of life in the army are to some extent misleading in that they were amongst the most imaginative and best educated of the common soldiers, but they did not consider themselves to be creatures apart, or complain about the vast majority of their comrades, and they were all proud of the army and unquenchably loyal to their regiments.

Most of their books are full of the hardships and occasional recreations of the soldier on compaign, and are confined to the world immediately around him, in which finding a pair of boots is as important as the fall of a besieged town. Sergeant Stevenson had a more serious purpose in describing his twenty-one years in the army. He was a deeply religious man who had found God some time after he had enlisted, and although he was the first to acknowledge that the army was no school of virtue, he was concerned that his readers should not believe the horrors they read about in the newspapers. He mentions his own awakening to religion, and the many devout soldiers he knew, and claims that any young fellow might preserve his good character in the army.

4   *Private of the 42nd Regiment*

5   *Grenadier of the 1st Regiment of Guards*

6   *Rifleman*

7   *Private of the Life Guards*

8   *Hussar*

From William Alexander, "Picturesque Representations of the Dress and Manners of the English", 1817

9   *Lord Uxbridge*

10   *Sir Thomas Picton*

Both from Christopher Kelly, "The Memorable Battle of Waterloo", 1817

He thought it the finest career a man might follow, as well as one which offered excellent conditions compared with civilian life. Of greater significance was Stevenson's attempt to nail the lie that the army was officered by brutes and disciplined by savage floggings, and the heatedness of his argument on this point suggests that the army had gained such a reputation quite early on. He cites the number of responsible and considerate officers he had met, and argues that not only were courts martial anxious to avoid floggings, but that they awarded comparatively few. The savagery of the contemporary civil penal code strengthened Stevenson's contention that the army was a reasonably humane institution.*

Stevenson's reservations reduce the grisly legends of military punishment to more creditable proportions, but appallingly brutal sentences were nevertheless common. Sergeant Lawrence's auto-biography records that a soldier he reported for cowardice at Waterloo received 300 strokes, well administered by the drummers. The victim spent three weeks in hospital recovering from his injuries. The details Lawrence gives of his later career are even more horrifying. For various offences, including selling his kit, he received three more floggings each of 300 strokes, after which he was expelled in disgrace from the regiment in an impressive and painful ceremony. Sentences of 1,000 strokes were awarded in 1815 for robbery.

The distance between officers and men in the army of 1815 was far greater than it is today, but offered fewer causes of tension and resentment because it was bridged by the usages of a still largely traditional society. At its best their relationship was that of the considerate squire and his villagers, for the great majority of recruits came from the land, just as the officers were mostly drawn from good country families. The towns of early nineteenth-century England were too small and too few to exert any more influence on the army than they did on the civil population. Communications were still rudimentary, and although literacy was more widespread than is generally supposed, reading matter was very limited in quantity and scope. Village life was largely self-contained, and in many respects hardly more self-conscious than it had been for

* Corporal punishment did not exist in the Imperial Army; the French were horrified by the barbarity of English discipline.

centuries. The distinctions of class and calling were sharply drawn, and the common soldier was accustomed to a degree of surveillance which ranged from the paternal to the tyrannical. The individual and his conscience had far more impact on those around him than they have today, when the development of social institutions has transferred so much personal responsibility to the state. Against the brutal and sadistic commanders of whom we read we should place the large proportion of officers who endeared themselves to their men.

In such a context officers were able to call men by their christian names, and join them in games without feeling any sense of strain. Sergeant Morris of the 73rd records as quite the most natural thing that some of the officers and men were playing ball against the gable-end of one of the village houses when their orders came to march to Quatre Bras. In the 'nineties of the previous century the future Duke of Richmond recommended himself to his regiment by being the only officer who bothered to share in the men's games of cricket. The officers and men of one infantry regiment stationed in North America relieved the tedium of the winter months of 1814 by improvising a theatre and producing a play. There is some irony in the fact that the apparently rigid social system of the Regency should have had far less tendency than our own to place people in arbitrary and stultifying categories; for although commissions were customarily by purchase, and largely the prerogative of the gentry, a small but steady number of N.C.O.s were able to become officers. Sergeant Morris's description of one of his comrades suggests that in a good regiment the soldier's life was far from oppressive:

> "Among the list of the killed, on the 18th, was poor Jack Parsons, one of the best hearted, good-humoured, generous fellows that I ever met with. He was a native of Staffordshire, and invariably carried with him, in his knapsack, the last gift of his poor old mother, consisting of a piece of bacon, which he preserved with as much care as if it had been the most valuable relic.
>
> Poor Jack was so fond of drink, that he was always getting into some scrape, and passed a great deal of his time in the guard-room, as a prisoner. His frolics, however, when inebriated, were of so perfectly good-humoured and harmless a nature that he never received any more severe punishment than con-

finement to the guard-room, with extra guards, drills, and stoppage of grog—the last, to him the worst punishment of all.

When any of the men were to be deprived of their grog, it was generally spilt in the front of the company; and on one occasion, as the officer was in the act of turning out Jack's allowance from a canteen, the poor fellow cast an anxious glance at the precious liquid, as it trickled on the ground, and adopted the following expedient to save, at least a portion of it. Turning his eyes in a direction behind the officer, he said, 'Here's the general coming, Sir'; the officer turned sharply round to see where, and in the meantime Jack had both hands under the canteen, receiving as much as they would contain, and conveying to his mouth. The officer could not help laughing at the ingenuity of the trick, and generously returned him the canteen, with a portion of the spirit remaining in it.

On another occasion, when marching through Germany, we were for some days without our usual supply of spirits, from the utter inability of the quartermaster to obtain it. Some German Hussars were marching in the same direction with us, and as usual with them on the line of march, were singing in chorus. Our colonel not being acquainted with the German language said to an officer, with whom he was riding, 'I wonder what they are singing about?' Jack immediately replied in the hearing of the colonel, 'I know what they are singing about!' 'Well, Jack,' said the colonel, 'Let's hear what it is.' 'Why,' said Jack, 'they are singing—

'We have got sch–n–a–a–ps,
And the 73rd have got no–o–one.'

The hint was not thrown away, for the colonel said laughing, 'Well, Jack, we'll try and get you some schnaps tonight.'"

The authors of the letters and reminiscences which describe the ordinary soldier's life were convinced that they belonged to the finest regiments in the army, and the intensity of their loyalty owed much to the fact that the regiment was virtually their home and family. Leave was granted infrequently, at the end of campaigns and tours of duty, and their families were usually too far away to be visited. Sergeant Lawrence did not see his village in Dorset for sixteen years. Two years after Waterloo, when he was garrisoned in Scotland, he was given six weeks' leave. He and his wife, a French girl he married while serving in the army of occupation, decided to undertake the long journey to visit his parents. They were able to take a coastal packet as far as London, and walked or rode in a cart for the rest of the way. They returned to Scotland

49

on foot, having spent in all three weeks on the road. For some time afterwards, remarks Sergeant Lawrence briefly, his wife's feet suffered from the frostbite she contracted towards the end of their tramp back to Scotland.

In 1815 a sergeant's pay was 13*d*. per day, of which 6*d*. was deducted to meet the cost of his food. His earnings, taken together with his lodging and other emoluments in kind, compared quite favourably with the average farm labourer's wage of 10*s*. per week. On retirement he might be given as much as 9*d*. per day pension, 3*d*. more than a private, which he would supplement by taking a job. At times the troops received large lump sums; when a number of sergeants were paid the arrears which had accumulated during the Peninsula campaigns the amounts varied from £40 to £60. A sergeant's prize money for Waterloo was nearly £20. Most soldiers frittered away these occasional windfalls in a few weeks' amusement; their lives discouraged thrift. Normal pay went largely on drink and tobacco, recreations which figure continually as the highlights in campaigners' recollections. For the vast majority of Wellington's army the daily issue of spirits was as welcome as its value in cash.

From time to time the troops had the opportunity to collect money and valuables from the dead and wounded enemy on the battlefield. Elsewhere the penalties for pillaging were so savage that the English enjoyed an admirable if unrewarding reputation abroad as the only army which did not leave a trail of destruction in its wake. Wellington was particularly insistent on this, lent a ready ear to complaints, and executed men found guilty of looting. The French were unable to impose such restrictions because, unlike the English, they made no attempt to supply their soldiers with regular and adequate rations. In 1814 French troops lived for the first time off their own land; when Wellington's troops advanced into the south of France they were welcomed with relief. Meanwhile, in the north, the Prussians took what the retreating French had left untouched; they were avenging themselves for the Emperor's endless campaigns in Germany.

The French infantrymen showed far more ingenuity and resource than the English in looking after themselves in the field. They excelled in constructing bivouacs from improbable materials, while the English were content with makeshifts. The French were frugal eaters, and saved as much food as they could if they thought that there was much chance of going short within the next few days. It was said of Wellington's men that if they were given sufficient rations for five days, few of them would have a scrap left by the end of the second day. No doubt the soldier accompanied by his wife made more effort.

The War Office had little alternative to allowing women to accompany their husbands on active service. Recruits were required to spend such long periods away from home that it would have been impossible to find volunteers for the army if they were not permitted to marry after a number of years with the colours. The authorities made every attempt to minimise the number of wives going on campaign, and on embarkation they enforced a strict quota system which left many desperate women on the quay. The fortunate ones suffered all the privations of the field. They marched with the army to the battlefield, where they tended the wounded in the rear.* Many followed their husbands from devotion, and left the army if their partners were killed. Others were content to remarry, and some were unlucky enough to be widowed several times during the Peninsular Campaigns. Although a large proportion were certainly promiscuous, faithful wives were treated honourably by their husbands' comrades. Amongst women prepared to undergo unremitting hardships were a number of striking personalities who became widely known and loved, and whose presence went far to redeem the harshness and tedium of campaign. The strongest bonds of love and companionship united the couples whose marriages survived, and the quality of their relationship shines out in the accounts such husbands left.

Sometimes at a discreeter distance, but often as hardily, a smaller proportion of officers' wives accompanied the army. Like the wives of privates and N.C.O.s, they were exposed to the hazards of pregnancy far from home and reasonable conditions, and Mrs. Deacon, the wife of an ensign in Sergeant Morris's regiment, the 73rd Foot, endured quite as much anxiety and suffering as any in

* At least two of the wives at Waterloo were wounded when attempting to bring their injured husbands off the battlefield.

the brief campaign of 1815. Her husband was wounded in the arm
at Quatre Bras:

> "After getting his wound dressed, he went in search of his
> wife, who, with her three children, he had left with the baggage
> guard. During the whole night, he sought her in vain; and
> the exertion he used was more than he could bear, and he was
> conveyed by the baggage train to Brussels.
>
> The poor wife, in the meantime, who had heard from some
> of the men that her husband was wounded, passed the whole
> night in searching for him among the wounded, as they passed.
> At length, she was informed that he had been conveyed to
> Brussels and her chief anxiety then was how to get there.
> Conveyances there were not to be got; and she was in the last
> stage of pregnancy; but, encouraged by the hope of finding
> her husband, she made the best of her way on foot, with her
> children, exposed to the violence of the terrific storm of thunder,
> lightning, and rain, which continued unabated for about ten
> hours. Faint, exhausted, and wet to the skin, having no clothes
> than a black silk dress, and light shawl, yet, she happily sur-
> mounted all these difficulties; reached Brussels on the morning
> of the 18th; and found her husband in very comfortable
> quarters, where she also was accommodated; and the next day
> gave birth to a fine girl, which was afterwards christened
> 'Waterloo Deacon'."

4

Ligny and Quatre Bras

"THE THREE DAYS' FIGHT IS OVER", Sergeant Wheeler wrote in a letter home as his regiment marched towards Paris after the Battle of Waterloo. To the soldiers who took part in the campaign there seemed to be little distinction between Waterloo and the battles which they fought two days before at Ligny and Quatre Bras. It was early on the morning of Thursday, the 15th of June, that the first squadrons of French light cavalry crossed the frontier into Belgium and set off down the road to Charleroi; close behind them followed the rest of the army.

Napoleon had achieved complete surprise over Blücher and Wellington, whose armies were too widely scattered to offer serious resistance. By the evening of the first day of the campaign the Emperor's army was placed between the allies, who were still struggling to concentrate their forces. On Friday the 16th the French fought two battles, one at Ligny against the Prussians, the other at Quatre Bras against the English. On the 17th Napoleon pursued the English to the Waterloo position, where on Sunday, the 18th, the last battle of the campaign took place. In ninety-seven hours overwhelming French success had been transformed into disaster, Napoleon had threatened Brussels and lost all chance of holding Paris. There could have been no more ironical conclusion to the career of the man who had taught Europe that a short campaign, a single pitched battle, were sufficient to bring his army into an enemy's capital. Yet the completeness of Wellington's victory on the 18th is no more remarkable than the brilliance with which Napoleon opened the campaign four days before; in all his nineteen years as a commander in chief there is no more striking example of how to seize the initiative against superior forces and with it threaten their prompt destruction. The seeds of the defeat at Waterloo are not to be found in the Emperor's plan of campaign or even the execution of its first stages, but in a succession of blunders and omissions, some of them his own, some of them his subordinates'.

The tremendous reversal of fortune at Waterloo has eclipsed Quatre Bras and Ligny, and the strategy which gave rise to them, just as it has redeemed Wellington's grossest errors. Yet without the events of the 15th, Ligny and Quatre Bras, Waterloo is no more than *Hamlet* without the Prince; it is against the background of the entire campaign that the last decisive battle takes on its full interest and importance.

On the 3rd of June, less than a fortnight before the campaign was due to begin, Napoleon issued orders for the concentration of the Army of the North in the area bounded by Maubeuge, Avesnes, Rocroi and Chimay.* Complete surprise was essential to the Emperor's plan to defeat the superior allied forces. He had to mass his army and throw it against the enemy's advanced posts before the alarm was given. While Blücher and Wellington attempted to concentrate their armies the French should be able to deal one or even both of them a crippling blow, the balance of strength would be tipped in Napoleon's favour, and his forces would be poised for the occupation of Brussels and the rest of Belgium. In ten days 124,000 men were assembled on the start line from distances which varied from 30 to 200 miles. This remarkable achievement would have gone for nothing if news of the troops' movements had leaked out on even the last day of the operation; twenty-four hours would have been sufficient for the allies to gather together enough forces to hold up the invasion until the rest of their troops arrived to rob the Emperor of the initiative. The secret was well preserved; the French army was massed within an hour's march of the allied lines while the English and Prussians were still completely unaware of the storm that was about to burst over their heads. The two armies lay dispersed over an area of 135 miles, and to concentrate on the centre of their lines, where the armies joined, would take them three days; a week would be needed to assemble all the allied troops on either wing. The Emperor's orders to march

* Chimay did not become Belgian until the peace treaty of 1815.

were accompanied by instructions to cut all communications across the border. Works were started along stretches of the frontier to strengthen the allies' assumption that the French must remain on the defensive, and as the troops of the Army of the North left frontier posts their places were taken unobtrusively by the National Guard. By presuming that an attack against their superior forces was almost impossible Blücher and Wellington made it virtually inevitable. For Napoleon to remain on the defensive was out of character; they cannot have taken account of this, for had they done so they would not have left themselves so open to surprise and defeat. In the circumstances, once Napoleon had gathered his army together without discovery at the weakest point in his enemy's line, the junction of the two scattered armies, his initial success was guaranteed.

Detachments of the Guard, the last troops in the capital to join the army, left Paris on the eighth of June. Two days later Napoleon went to the theatre for the last time; he saw Talma appear at the Théâtre Français in a feeble tragedy called *Hector*, by Luce de Lancival. He was greeted by an immense ovation as he entered his red-draped box. A witness describes how Napoleon, obliged to acknowledge his reception, "half rose, leaning towards us, and rewarded our cries with a smile that has remained for ever in my memory". The next day, the 11th, was a Sunday; a week before Waterloo. The Emperor heard mass at the Tuileries for the last time, and afterwards gave several audiences. A number of letters were dictated, one of them to Davout, concerning Ney.

The Emperor had decided to relieve the Marshal of his disgrace and give him a command in the forthcoming campaign. The fact that Ney would be plunged immediately into active operations with an unfamiliar staff and troops he would not have time to get to know, scarcely seems to have troubled Napoleon. The Emperor had lost confidence in Ney's grasp of any strategical situation years before, and the reasons for his decision to employ him again must remain obscure; it is not very likely that he was moved by compassion at the downfall of the hero of the Russian Campaign. He may have thought that Ney's fighting experience would be of more than usual value in an army which lacked commanders used to heavy responsibility. Napoleon may not have intended to give Ney the important rôle that fell upon him during the Waterloo Campaign: Marshal Mortier, an infinitely sounder general, was also joining the army. The timing of the Emperor's summons suggests that he gave way to personal rather than practical considerations: tell Ney, he wrote to Davout, to meet me at Avesnes "if he wishes to be present at the first battles."

It was not long before the Emperor regretted this decision. Letter writing at an end, Napoleon took a walk in the garden, because his "head was bursting", and then dined with his mother and brothers. At four o'clock the next morning he left the Elysée and drove to Soissons where he stopped for lunch; the night was passed at Laon. On the 13th of June he slept at Avesnes. On the evening of Wednesday, the 14th of June, the Emperor moved his headquarters to Beaumont, at the centre of the army, whose concentration was now virtually complete. His orders had been fulfilled almost to the letter, the army had assembled on time; early next morning the machine would be launched at the allied armies.

A few miles away lay the Belgian frontier; behind it scattered far and wide were the English and Prussian cantonments. There was no sense of urgency in the allied lines, no suspicion that within a matter of hours the two armies would be at grips with the French; their normal round of occupations and amusements continued. In the intervals between training and preparing for a succession of reviews Wellington's men passed their time in smoking and drinking, visiting neighbouring villages, wandering through the streets of nearby towns, occasionally quarrelling with the Belgians, but on the whole receiving a generous measure of hospitality. Their officers shared even more in this convivial atmosphere.

They enjoyed an active social round in Brussels, where many of their wives and families had arrived to join them together with English visitors attracted partly by the forthcoming campaign and partly by the novelty of being able to visit the Continent after so many years of confinement. Wellington shared their amusements to the full. Rumours reached the Duke on the 12th that Napoleon was at Maubeuge, but he paid so little attention to the possibility that he went off to Enghien for the day. Two letters of the Rev. Spencer Madan, tutor to the young Lennoxes, a family with whom the Duke was particularly friendly, show something of Wellington during the last two days before the storm broke.

"Brussels, 13th June, 1815

"... Though I have some pretty good reasons for supposing that hostilities will soon commence, yet no one would suppose it, judging by the Duke of Wellington. He appears to be thinking of anything else in the world, gives a ball every week, attends every party, partakes of every amusement that offers. (Yesterday) he took Lady Jane Lennox to Enghien for the cricket match, and brought her back at night, apparently having gone for no other object but to amuse her. At the time Bonaparte was said to be at Maubeuge, thirty or forty miles off."

Wellington certainly did not think that hostilities would soon commence, and he wrote to Lord Lynedoch to say so, on the 13th, the day after his trip to Enghien, when Napoleon was supervising the final stages of his army's concentration. Fresh rumours of Napoleon's presence near the frontier were brought to Wellington's notice on the 14th, but he still took no action. "In the drawing-room before dinner", wrote Madan that day, "he was playing with the children, who seemed to look up to him as to one on whom they might depend for amusement. When dinner was announced they quitted him with great regret, saying, 'Be sure you remember to send for us the moment dinner is over', which he promised to do, and was as good as his word." The Duke's first orders to his army were not sent out until the 15th, when early that morning Napoleon had crossed the frontier and entered the allies' forward lines *en masse*.

On the evening of Tuesday, the 13th, reports began to come in to Zieten, commander of the Prussian Ist Corps, from his outposts on the Sambre saying that the lights of many bivouac fires could be seen around Beaumont. Zieten forwarded this alarming evidence of a French army in front of his position to Blücher, who received his despatch late on the fourteenth. Blücher promptly ordered his IInd, IIIrd and IVth Corps to march on Sombreffe. He sent instructions to Zieten to cover the concentration of the Prussian army by offering a stubborn resistance, and to fall back towards Fleurus if he should be attacked by strongly superior forces.

Of all the mistakes committed during the Waterloo Campaign none was more crass than Blücher's attempt at the outset to collect his troops in an area that was within easy reach of an enemy army massed to attack. No doubt he counted on the later support of Wellington's army, for the two commanders had agreed at Tirlemont the month before to come to the other's assistance, should either be attacked, but by the time the English appeared on the scene the damage would have been done. So grave was Blücher's error that at first Napoleon could not believe that the reports of his march on Sombreffe were true; such things were not done, even by the most pedestrian commanders. After a few hours it became quite clear that Blücher had ordered a forward concentration, and Napoleon determined to seize the chance offered him of ending the campaign within forty-eight hours of its beginning. The Emperor had planned the start of the invasion by assuming that his two opponents would observe the more elementary rules of war; if he succeeded in massing his army secretly and attacked the junction of their scattered forces, he would with one stroke oblige them to fall back, apart from each other, surrendering ground in order to gain time to complete their concentration. While they were thus striving to prepare to meet him he would be able to interfere with their operations, and although numerically inferior to the two armies acting together, he would be able to bring superior forces to bear against whichever he chose to attack, for he would have time to fight one before he had to meet the other. Such was his general plan; its developments were to wait upon events.

At three in the morning of Thursday, the 15th of June, the Emperor mounted his horse, and very soon the first French troops began to cross the frontier. The army's bivouacs were broken up at regular intervals throughout the rest of the night and early morning in order to ensure a smooth and uninterrupted advance on the enemy lines. Before each regiment marched off to take its place in one of the three great columns directed on Charleroi the men were assembled to hear the Emperor's order of the day. It reminded them that today was the anniversary of Marengo and Friedland; the coalition would enter France only to find its tomb; the moment had come for every Frenchman to conquer or die. During the early hours of the advance the army's pace was slowed by a thick mist which clung to the hollows and the wooded slopes,

11 *"The Artillery Officers had the range so accurately that every shot and shell fell into the very Centre of their Masses"*

12 *Battle of Quatre Bras. "The Square remained steady"*

Both from Captain Jones, "The Battle of Waterloo", 1816

13 *Marshal Soult*

From the portrait by George Peter Alexander Healy

but this dispersed as the sun rose above the horizon, giving way to a fine summer's day.

The three columns advanced towards Charleroi by different routes, so that they could come to each other's assistance if met by serious resistance. In the van were twelve regiments of cavalry, followed by three companies of engineers with fifteen pontoons and as many boats. The marching orders provided for the utmost flexibility and ease of movement; the ambulances were to join the column in the rear of the Emperor's staff, and any other vehicle which attempted to accompany the columns was to be burnt. Until further notice baggage and ammunition waggons were to remain at nine miles distance from the army. The commanders of the three advanced guards were instructed not to get ahead of each other, to send out scouts in every direction, to question the inhabitants about the enemy's positions and to seize all the letters in the post offices. They were to send frequent reports of their progress to the Emperor, who marched with the leading troops of the central column. By noon the bulk of the army would be across the Sambre.

The inhabitants of Charleroi were largely pro-French in sympathy, and they greeted the Emperor with considerable applause when he rode into the town soon after midday. He halted at a small inn called Belle-Vue, from which he could see far along the valley of the Sambre. He sent for a chair from the inn and sat down at the side of the road along which the infantry was marching. The troops' enthusiasm had reached the point of hysteria, and they passed the Emperor with great shouts of "*Vive l'Empereur!*"; some broke their ranks to embrace the Emperor's horse which stood by the roadside. Napoleon soon fell asleep in his chair despite the noise and excitement; he had been in the saddle since three that morning and had, moreover, been subject in Paris to fits of drowsiness during the spring and early summer.

The lights of the bivouac fires around Beaumont had warned the Prussians of impending attack; by morning they learnt how massive it was. At seven, General Bourmont, commander of the 14th Infantry Division, accompanied by his staff, rode into Zieten's lines to surrender himself and reveal Napoleon's strength and his plan of campaign. The news was taken as quickly as possible to

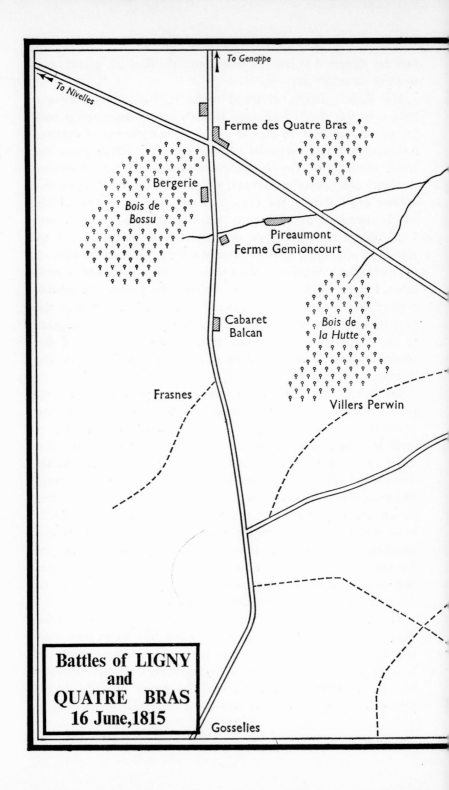

Battles of LIGNY
and
QUATRE BRAS
16 June, 1815

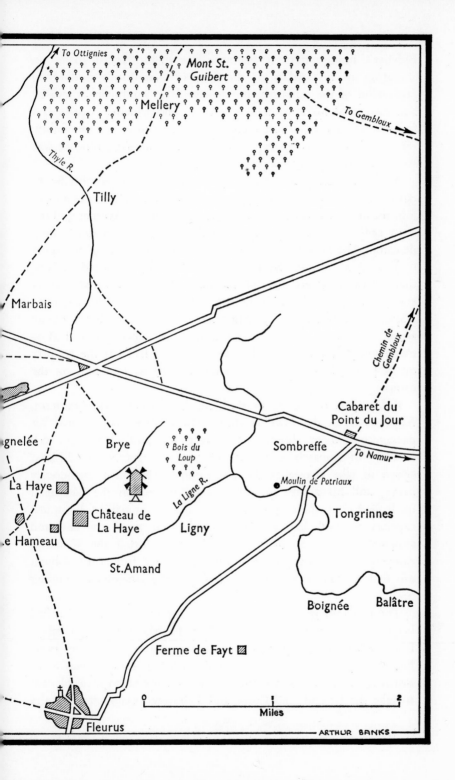

Blücher's headquarters at Namur. The Field-Marshal made no alteration to his orders in the face of Napoleon's undoubted possession of the initiative, but hastened to Sombreffe, where he had instructed his army to concentrate, and which he reached at four in the afternoon. Sustained by a belief in his own invincibility, remarkable even in the records of military optimism, Blücher was still determined to fight a pitched battle.

As the Prussian commander sped confidently to Sombreffe, an equally hot-headed soldier approached Charleroi. Ney's summons to join the army had been so late that he had reached Avesnes and the army only on the 13th, without his horses and only a single aide-de-camp. The next day he could find no other means of transport to Beaumont, where the Emperor had set up his headquarters, than a peasant's cart. On the morning of the 15th he was lucky enough to buy Mortier's horses, and with these he followed Napoleon to Charleroi. Mortier had been struck down by an attack of sciatica, which suggests that his subconscious had as much grasp of politics as the marshals who had left the country on Napoleon's return or who had declined to join him on the campaign.

Riding past the flanks of the columns marching on Charleroi, Ney arrived at the town at three. The soldiers had cheered his passage past them, shouting, "There is Redhead, all will go well now!" Unfortunately, of all possible commanders, Ney could least afford to take charge at the last minute. He was tremendously brave, and his ability to rally shaken troops on the battlefield unrivalled, but these qualities were not accompanied by much capacity to think logically. He would often wreck the best and simplest strategy, as he was to do again during the Waterloo campaign, and ten years before the exasperated Emperor had burst out that Ney knew less of his plans than the last-joined drummer boy.

The Emperor greeted Ney kindly on his arrival, although it had been only a few months before that the Marshal had promised Louis XVIII to bring back his former master in an iron cage. Napoleon put Ney in charge of the left wing; no time was to be lost if the French were to consolidate their initial surprise. He was to take the Ist and IInd Corps and Lefebvre-Desnouettes' cavalry division, and with them sweep the scattered enemy off the Charleroi-Brussels road. Quatre Bras was to be seized and occupied. A glance at the map will show how vital it was to secure the cross roads at Quatre Bras; they were the key to the whole strategic situation, for they controlled the communications between the English and Prussian armies. The events of the next few days would hinge on this hamlet, 11 miles from Charleroi. Whichever side held Quatre Bras would hamper the enemy's movements, and on the 15th of June it was not likely that there were more than a few isolated detachments of allied troops between Charleroi and the cross roads.

As Ney rode off to take over his command Grouchy joined the Emperor. Napoleon gave him the right wing of the army, the IIIrd and IVth Corps, with instructions to push the Prussians he should encounter towards Sombreffe. Grouchy set about the task so slowly that after a couple of hours the Emperor rode forward to hurry him on. An engagement with Zieten's outnumbered corps ensued, and in accordance with his instructions, the Prussian general fell back to Fleurus. Here the French right wing halted for the night. Ney moved even more slowly than Grouchy, and whatever the difficulties he found in taking charge of a wing of the army at such short notice, it is hard to understand the reascns for his delay when speed was at such a premium. He drove some Prussians out of Gosselies, three and a half miles from Charleroi, and there halted his infantry; thus he compromised his chances of taking Quatre Bras.

The last repercussions of this extraordinary decision will not die away until Waterloo itself has been forgotten. The Emperor's orders had been categoric on the need to capture the intersection of the roads leading from Brussels through Waterloo to Quatre Bras and from Quatre Bras via Sombreffe to Namur; leaving the road junction in the hands of the allies created totally unnecessary difficulties for the French. So important was Ney's objective that almost any risk might have been thought necessary to take it, although, of course, he was on the road in such strength that he ran scarcely any hazard at all in advancing to Quatre Bras before nightfall.

The Emperor's arrangements for the 15th of June were perfectly normal ones, and such operations had been commonplace in the French army for the last twenty years; Ney had not been asked to do anything complicated or dangerous. The Emperor had split up his army into the customary three groups within a few hours' march of each other to give them the maximum mobility with the maximum security. In this way each part was strong enough to hold off virtually any enemy forces it might meet at such short notice until the rest of the army could march to its relief.

Quatre Bras was well within the working distance of such a scheme and it was moreover extremely unlikely that Wellington had concentrated a quarter of the number Ney had with him. The Marshal's fatal delay on the afternoon of the 15th has been explained in a variety of ways by military historians, but none of them has produced a completely satisfactory reason. Most take the view that for once in his life, Ney yielded to prudence, a characteristic so rare in his campaigns that one hesitates to accept it as an argument; the distance he had been ordered to travel from the rest of the army was not so great that he was gravely endangering the forces under his command, even if it turned out that Wellington had got wind of the invasion and was marching to meet him with the whole of his army. What is more, Ney had been told to occupy Quatre Bras, and when Ney disobeyed orders it was from excess of zeal, not want of it.

Only slightly less satisfactory than the view that Ney failed to advance to Quatre Bras because he thought it was too dangerous an operation, is the suggestion that he did not grasp the significance of the cross roads. Yet the importance of Quatre Bras was so glaringly obvious that one of Wellington's subordinates disobeyed orders in order to occupy the hamlet with a small force. The fact that it is possible to doubt whether a general of Ney's experience understood the value of seizing Quatre Bras goes some way to indicate the difficulties of reading the mind of so odd and impulsive a personality.

Had Ney been inclined to imagine that Wellington was approaching his positions in force, his fears were groundless. When the French reached Gosselies, Wellington was still in Brussels, and he gave no orders for his army to concentrate until between five and seven that evening. For all that he was confronted by an offensive conducted by the ablest general of the era, the Duke continued to behave in an extraordinarily leisurely way. Having issued his belated instructions, he went off to the Duchess of Richmond's ball in Brussels with a sangfroid which was almost as unconscious as it was unjustified. If Ney had taken Quatre Bras Wellington would have arrived at the front next day in time to withdraw his forces, for by then the fate of Blücher's army would have been sealed, and the French left free to turn their superior numbers on the English.

Having halted his infantry at Gosselies, Ney sent Lefebvre-Desnouettes' cavalry division along the road. A squadron of Polish lancers which had left the body of the advanced guard rode up to Quatre Bras to find the cross roads unoccupied. The squadron commander decided to return to the main force; the position was too far from the rest of Ney's troops to be held with so few men, especially in so thoroughly confused a situation, where the enemy's outposts were falling back and his other troops coming forward to support them. He wheeled his squadron round and made off down the road to report to Ney. The Polish horsemen had not long left Quatre Bras before Prince Bernhard of Saxe-Weimar appeared at the cross roads with 4,500 infantry and a battery of six guns. He had heard accidentally at Genappe that the French had crossed the Sambre that morning, and it was on his own initiative that he ordered his small force to occupy Quatre Bras in face of the French. As Ney rode up to the front to look at the situation, Saxe-Weimar's men were occupying the buildings of the hamlet and the roads which ran past them.

Small though Saxe-Weimar's numbers were, Ney had only 1,700 cavalry and a solitary battalion of infantry within call. He abandoned any thought of taking Quatre Bras that evening, and a little after seven turned back towards Gosselies, where he was to pass the night. The Emperor had given Ney charge of over 50,000 men, and if he had sent forward only a quarter of them, say 14,000, from Gosselies at five o'clock, he would have swept away the last resistance at Quatre Bras before last light at nine o'clock. At such a stage in the campaign it is difficult to see what difficulties these 14,000 men could have got themselves into, still harder to imagine that the 35,000 troops within call could not have extricated them, had the need arisen. Possibly Ney had thought to make war by the book when he hung back from advancing in force on Quatre Bras, but all that he had done was to turn the book upside down.

In Brussels Wellington accomplished nothing constructive all day. In reality he made matters much worse by issuing totally inappropriate orders. Ever since his arrival in April he had been convinced that should Napoleon take the offensive it would be by way of Mons, a direction which would enable the French to fall on his communications with the sea. This was very muddled thinking; Napoleon's whole strategy was to force Wellington and Blücher apart, and a thrust towards the sea via Mons would drive the allied armies together, allowing them to meet him with superior forces. Not until midnight on the 15th did Wellington realise how badly he had appreciated Napoleon's strategical objectives and methods; meanwhile precious time had been lost. At three that afternoon the Duke received a despatch announcing that the Prussian outposts at Thuin had been driven in. Between five and seven he issued orders for his divisions to concentrate at the points already given them, that is, to meet an advance in the direction of Mons, and to be prepared to move from their concentration areas at the shortest notice.

These orders travelled slowly, and were out of date before they arrived. The instructions for the Prince of Orange's divisions reached his headquarters at eleven o'clock on the evening of the 15th. The Prince himself had set off for Brussels some hours before to attend the Duchess of Richmond's ball. Rebecque, the Chief of Staff, passed the message in silence to Perponcher, one of the divisional commanders. Perponcher's men were at Quatre Bras, where Saxe-Weimar, the brigade commander had taken them from Genappe that afternoon on his own initiative, when he had learnt of the French occupation of Charleroi and realised how essential it was to deny them if possible the roads which linked the allied armies.

Perponcher now held in his hand Wellington's order to move his troops to Nivelles; to obey would be to jeopardise the army, and he and Rebecque decided to ignore it; instead Saxe-Weimar was strengthened at the cross roads. By intelligent disobedience, first Saxe-Weimar, then Perponcher and Rebecque had thrown a barrier across the Brussels road behind which the rest of Welling-ton's army could gather to meet the real direction of the invasion, via Charleroi, not Mons. More important still, the presence of allied troops at Quatre Bras prevented Napoleon from carrying out the destruction of the Prussian army next day. Instead of marching his troops to Quatre Bras and taking the right-hand road to fall on the flank of Blücher's army as the Emperor overwhelmed its front, Ney was to spend his efforts against Wellington. Without Ney's assistance, the Emperor failed to crush the Prussians, and when he joined Ney to attack the English at Waterloo, Blücher's army was able to rob him of his victory.

The hours continued to pass in Brussels without Wellington's seeing the situation in its true light. Earlier in the evening a message arrived from Blücher saying that he was concentrating his army at Sombreffe. Despite the Tirlemont agreement to come to Blücher's assistance, the Duke remained so apprehensive of a thrust past his right flank that he considered it his first duty to cover the roads from Mons and Ath to Brussels, and a second set of orders were sent off at 10 p.m. to see that this was done. Unaware that he had thus confounded confusion, the Duke left for the Duchess of Richmond's ball where he was to stay until two that morning. Wellington thought that in the circumstances he and his officers would do best to attend the ball and stiffen civilian morale.

At midnight a long-delayed despatch from Mons removed the scales from Wellington's eyes. The garrison commander, General Dornberg, reported that Napoleon had moved with all his forces on Charleroi and that there was no sign of the enemy in front. Convinced at last that his right flank was safe, the Duke ordered the whole army to march on Quatre Bras. Wellington saw at once how great his mistake had been, as the conversation with his host a few minutes later bears out. This the Duke of Richmond repeated immediately afterwards to Captain Bowles, whose account of the episode is printed in Malmesbury's *Letters*:

> "The Duke of Wellington ... said to the Duke of Richmond, 'I think it is time for me to go to bed likewise'; and then, whilst wishing him good night, whispered to ask him if he had a good map in his house. The Duke of Richmond said he had, and took him into his dressing-room, which opened into the supper-room. The Duke of Wellington shut the door and

said, 'Napoleon had *humbugged* me, by G——! he has gained twenty-four hours on me.' The Duke of Richmond said, 'What do you intend doing?' The Duke of Wellington replied, 'I have ordered the army to concentrate at Quatre Bras; but we shan't stop him there, and if so, I must fight him *here*' (at the same time passing his thumbnail over the position of Waterloo). He then said adieu, and left the house by another way out. He went to his quarters, slept six hours, and breakfasted, and rode at speed to Quatre Bras."

It was not until nine that evening that Napoleon returned to Charleroi from his visit to Grouchy's lines. He went straight to his bed, for he had risen at 3 a.m. and had spent much of the day on horseback. The Emperor had achieved his first objective, the separation of the allied armies, but his next step was still not clear; he did not yet know that Blücher had decided to bring him to battle the following day, or that Ney had failed to occupy Quatre Bras. Around him, in an area ten miles square, the French army lay in three columns, ready to manœuvre against either the English or the Prussians, and within easy reach of the road to Brussels should the allies continue to retire. At midnight the Emperor's sleep was interrupted by Ney, who stayed until two. Over supper he gave the Marshal fresh instructions, and must have stressed the importance of blocking the communications between Wellington and Blücher at Quatre Bras, if the French were to hope to meet only one enemy at a time.

The Emperor had no more than five hours sleep on the night of the 15th, for at 4 a.m. he rose once more. He was anxious to reach Brussels as soon as possible, and he decided to concentrate his efforts on the 16th against Wellington, whose army lay before the city. Should the Duke not make a stand in front of Brussels the Emperor was resolved to drive him back on Antwerp, still farther from Blücher, who was based on Liége. Before the bulk of the army could be swung against Wellington along the Charleroi-Brussels road, however, the Emperor had to ensure that Blücher could not march to join him, and to do this the Prussian rearguard under Zieten must be pushed back well beyond Gembloux, so that Blücher could not use the Namur-Wavre-Brussels road. By six the Emperor had issued orders to Ney and Grouchy to execute this plan. Grouchy was instructed to attack any Prussians he met at

Sombreffe or Gembloux; once Grouchy had reached Gembloux the Emperor would take his reserves and join Ney against Wellington. Napoleon repeated this straightforward scheme in his letter to Ney, adding that the Marshal was to be prepared to march on Brussels the moment the reserves from Gembloux had joined him; in the meantime he was to send one division over to Marbais to link up with Grouchy's left, hold six divisions at Quatre Bras, and post one five miles north of the cross roads.

At eight a despatch arrived from Grouchy which suggested that the Emperor's plan to push the Prussians past Gembloux and then turn on Wellington would have to be abandoned; strong forces were marching on Sombreffe from the direction of Namur. Blücher's army was, of course, accomplishing its concentration at Sombreffe, but the Emperor could hardly dare to hope that this was actually the case, and he set off to see for himself exactly what this totally unexpected development might mean. He reached Fleurus shortly before eleven, where he learnt to his annoyance that owing to clumsy staff work Gérard's corps, a substantial part of Grouchy's force, was still far in the rear, and would not arrive for another two hours. The Emperor went forward to examine the Prussian movements. At the north end of the town of Fleurus stood a tower-shaped brick-mill, from which the whole of the area could be seen, and having ordered some sappers to knock a hole in the circular roof and provide a platform to stand on, Napoleon ascended to survey the situation. A glance was sufficient to assure him that Blücher was bringing up his entire army; he had concentrated forward in spite of the rules and the Emperor descended from his observation post determined to defeat the Prussian army that afternoon. Blücher had solved the problem of separating the allies for him.

Unfortunately, two hours had to pass before the battle could begin, for it was not until one o'clock, as Blücher deployed his last corps, that Gérard's corps arrived. Although the Emperor did not know that Wellington's army was still so disorganised, he could be sure that on the afternoon of the 16th the English could not intervene. With Ney at Quatre Bras, their communications with Blücher would be severed, and what was more, Ney should be able to hold them off with a minimum of forces, while the remainder of his troops would be free to march from Quatre Bras to attack the Prussians in the flank and rear. There was every chance that these reinforcements would enter the battle as Napoleon drove the Prussians back from their front, and with their arrival Blücher's destruction was assured.

The Emperor's strategy was based on the reasonable assumption that Ney had wasted no time on the morning of the 16th to redeem his failure to take Quatre Bras on the 15th. No doubt Napoleon had underlined the need to occupy the cross roads during his midnight supper with Ney, and his first instructions at six next morning had been to place six divisions at Quatre Bras, and one five miles farther north. Ney's orders obliged him to overcome whatever resistance the allies might offer at the cross roads, and for this he had ample forces.

The Marshal, however, had done nothing that morning; no orders had been given, and as a result his forces were still scattered for miles behind his outposts. His first action should have been to march on Quatre Bras with the troops he had nearby, while the divisions in the rear hastened to catch up with him. Instead, the hours had passed while Ney remained sunk in apathy, and it was not until the Emperor's 6 a.m. despatch reached him at eleven that he issued any instructions.

The results of Ney's inactivity were grave, but they would have been disastrous if Wellington had appreciated the situation correctly the day before. Had the Duke's forces been sent orders to concentrate on Quatre Bras at 5 p.m. on the 15th of June, and not at midnight, when they had already received and executed instructions to march in another direction, Ney's fate would have been sealed by the time he reached Quatre Bras on the afternoon of the 16th. It is even possible that Wellington might have wheeled his army to the left at Quatre Bras and arrived to overwhelm Napoleon as his army came to grips with the Prussians. The simplest plans in war are rarely achieved, and the situation at Quatre Bras on the afternoon of the 16th degenerated into a stalemate, which cost both sides several thousand lives and the Emperor his decisive victory over the Prussians. Napoleon cannot be blamed for attempting an over-ambitious strategy; he was not seeking to defeat two armies in one day, as some critics have suggested. Nor was he asking too much of Ney; an average general would have grasped the Emperor's intentions, and all Ney was asked to do was to carry out a number of straightforward orders.

Wellington's forces made their several ways to Quatre Bras in utmost confusion; some of his regiments had received orders, others had not. Many of the first regiments to take the road were reached by the couriers bearing Wellington's altered instructions, the remainder continued to march towards their original destinations, until a chance encounter on the road and a hurried consultation put them *en route* for Quatre Bras. The majority of Wellington's forces had long journeys to the battlefield, and most of those who made detours in response to his mistaken early instructions arrived too late to join the battle. The experience of Sergeant Morris of the 73rd Foot is typical of the troops who did take part in the fighting at Quatre Bras:

> "On June 15th", he writes, "some of the officers and men were playing at ball, against the gable end of a house in the village, when an orderly dragoon brought dispatches from General Halket ... ordering us to fall in immediately and proceed to the town of Soignes. The men were scattered about variously engaged; but they soon understood, from the roll of the drums and the tone of the bugles, that their attendance was immediately necessary, in marching order. At four o'clock the order came, and by six we had fallen in and were off."

Morris's regiment marched twenty-seven miles to reach the field at three the next afternoon. Some of the officers who attended the Duchess of Richmond's ball had no time to change, and appeared at Quatre Bras still wearing ball dress. Captain Mercer's battery was several miles from the battle when

> "a cabriolet, drawing at a smart pace, passed us. In it was seated an officer of the Guards, coat open and snuff box in hand. I could not but admire the perfect nonchalance with which my man was thus hurrying forward to join in a bloody combat—much, perhaps, in the same manner, though certainly not in the same costume, as he might drive to Epsom or Ascot Heath."

Wellington set out from Brussels a little after seven that morning and reached the cross roads at ten. The only forces there were Saxe-Weimar's brigade and the rest of Perponcher's division, and they had occupied the hamlet in disobedience of the Duke's first orders. All was still quiet, for Ney did not begin to move his troops until an hour later, but if he had carried out the Emperor's instructions Wellington would have paid heavily for his blunders on the previous day. Having inspected the position, the Duke wrote to Blücher to inform him of his arrangements.

Time passed without any sign of a French attack, and Wellington judged it safe to ride over to see the Prussian commander for himself. It was one o'clock when they met at the Bussy windmill, from which they could see the two armies and Gérard's corps arriving to join the Emperor. Blücher was optimistic of his chances, but was naturally anxious to have Wellington's support. The Duke promised to assist him if not attacked himself at Quatre Bras. Blücher's troops were drawn up on the forward slope of a hill, and Wellington could not conceal his surprise that they were left exposed to the full force of the French artillery, for his own practice was to shelter his men behind a reverse slope during the preliminary bombardment and not bring them into sight until the enemy cavalry and infantry came up. "Everyone knows his own best", he remarked to Blücher, "but if I were to fight with mine here, I should expect to be beat." "My men like to see the enemy", Blücher retorted, but Wellington went away unconvinced. His military attaché at the Prussian headquarters asked the Duke what he thought of Blücher's deployment: "If they fight here they will be damnably mauled", he was told.

The meeting lasted little more than an hour, and by three Wellington returned to Quatre Bras to find his troops in a critical position. Ney had woken from his trance when the Emperor's orders arrived at eleven that morning; within three-quarters of an hour Reille's corps was on the road to Quatre Bras. The march was a short one, and a little before two o'clock Ney asked Reille to clear the enemy out of the woods south of the cross roads. Reille had fought the English in Spain, and was perfectly familiar with Wellington's practice of hiding his troops until the last moment; he was sure that the numbers of enemy he could see ahead bore no relation to their real strength.

He warned Ney of the dangers of a "Spanish battle", and Ney, who until then had thought that the occupation of Quatre Bras would be a simple affair, agreed that they should proceed with great caution. This decision saved the cross roads for Wellington because at two o'clock he was still without reinforcements, and all he had to meet the coming attack were the Prince of Orange's original 7,800 infantry, 50 horsemen and 14 guns. Ney was unable to profit from the Duke's mistakes because he had failed to take the normal precaution that morning of sending out patrols to reconnoitre Quatre Bras; when Reille suggested that he might find the whole of the English army before him, he had no means of knowing how inadequate Wellington's forces were. Within call were 19,000 French infantry, 3,000 cavalry and 60 guns, and a determined attack on the cross roads at two o'clock would have overwhelmed the defenders before help could reach them. As every minute passed, however, the rest of Wellington's army drew nearer, and before long Ney was outnumbered. Boldness early in the afternoon would have obliged Wellington to retreat, rather than risk the defeat of his forces in detail as they arrived at Quatre Bras, and the outcome of the 16th of June, and therefore the campaign, would have been far different. The French began a deliberate advance, and when Wellington returned to the scene at three o'clock his situation was desperate; it was retrieved by the appearance of Picton's division and a brigade of cavalry. These reinforcements preserved the crumbling English front, and when the Duke of Brunswick's Corps joined them soon afterwards Reille's troops were slightly outnumbered.

The Brunswickers were well in advance of most of Wellington's army, and at nightfall many regiments were still far from the battlefield. Captain Mercer's battery arrived just too late to be useful, but his journal deserves quotation for its description of the conditions behind Quatre Bras. His men had to make their way through the confusion of the baggage trains, the stragglers, the wounded, and the deserters.

"A most extensive view lay before us; and now for the first time, as emerging from the woods, we became sensible of a dull, sullen sound that filled the air, somewhat resembling that of a distant water-mill, or still more distant thunder.

"By-and-by a large town appeared in front of us, and the increasing intensity of the cannonade, the volumes of smoke about the trees, led us to suppose the battle near at hand, and on the hill just beyond the town. This town was Nivelle. . . .

"Before entering the town we halted for a moment, lighted our slow matches, put shot into our leathern cartouches, loaded the guns with powder, and stuck priming wires into the vents to prevent the cartridges slipping forward, and thus prepared for immediate action, again moved on.

"The whole population of Nivelle was in the streets, doors and windows all wide open, whilst the inmates of the houses, male and female, stood huddled together in little groups like frightened sheep, or were hurrying along with the distracted air of people uncertain where they are going, or what they are doing. . . . In a sort of square which we traversed, a few soldiers, with the air of citizens (probably a municipal guard), were drawn up in line, looking anxiously about them at the numerous bleeding figures we now began to meet. Some were staggering along unaided, the blood falling from them in large drops as they went. One man we met was wounded in the head; pale and ghastly, with affrighted looks and uncertain step, he evidently knew little of where he was, or what passed about him, though still he staggered forward, the blood streaming down his face on to the greatcoat he wore rolled over his left shoulder. An anxious crowd was collecting round him as we passed on. Then came others supported between two comrades, their faces deadly pale, the knees yielding at every step. At every step, in short, we met numbers, more or less wounded, hurrying along in search of . . . assistance. Priests were running to and fro, hastening to assist at the last moments of a dying man; all were in haste—all wore that abstracted look so inseparable from those engaged in an absorbing pursuit.

"The road was covered with soldiers, many of them wounded, but also many apparently untouched. The numbers thus leaving the field appeared extraordinary. Many of the wounded had six, eight, ten or even more, attendants. When questioned about the battle, and why they left it, the answer was invariably, "*Monsieur, tout est perdu! les Anglais sont abimés, en déroute, abimés, tous, tous, tous!*" and then, nothing abashed, these fellows would resume their hurried route. My countrymen will rejoice to learn that amongst this dastardly crew not one Briton appeared. Whether they were of Nassau or Belgians, I know not; they were one or the other—I think the latter.

"One red-coat we did meet—not a fugitive though, for he was severely wounded . . . I stopped to ask news of the battle, telling him what I had heard from the others. 'Na, na, Sir, it's aw a damned lee; they were fechtin yat an a laft 'em; but it's a bludy business, and thar's na saying what may be the end on't. Oor ragiment was nigh clean swapt off, and oor Colonel kilt jist as I cam awa'.' A little further on, and as it began to grow dusk, we traversed the village of Hautain le Val, where a very different scene presented itself. Here, in a large cabaret by the roadside, we saw through the open windows the rooms filled with soldiers, cavalry and infantry; some standing about in earnest conversation, others seated round tables, smoking,

14 *"Bonaparte in his retreat passing La Belle Alliance"*

15 *"The perilous situation of Marshal Blücher at the Battle of Ligny"* (see p. 87)

Both from Christopher Kelly, "The Memorable Battle of Waterloo", 1817

16 *von Gneisenau*

From the portrait by George Dawe

17 *Gérard*

From a lithograph by Delpech

carousing and thumping the board with clenched fists, as they
related in loud voices—what?—most likely their own gallant
exploits. About the door their poor horses, tied to a rail, showed
by their drooping heads, shifting legs and the sweat drying
and fuming on their soiled coats, that their exertions at least
had been of no trivial nature.

"The firing began to grow slacker, and even intermitting,
as we entered on the field of Quatre Bras—our horses stumbling
from time to time over corpses of the slain, which they were
too tired to step over. The shot and shells which flew over our
line of march from time to time (some of the latter bursting
beyond us) were sufficient to enable us to say we had been *in*
the battle of Quatre Bras, for such was the name of the place
where we had now arrived, just too late to be useful."

Eight miles from Quatre Bras the battle of Ligny began just
before three o'clock. The start had been delayed while Gérard's
corps joined the Emperor, and this allowed Blücher to deploy
his last detachments. The Prussian commander had occupied a
string of villages and hamlets* which lay along the course of the
Ligne, a winding stream fifteen to twenty feet in breadth and three
to four feet deep, bordered by willows, alder trees and bramble
bushes. In the centre of the line, and most important of all, was
the village of Ligny, with its two large farms, old castle, church
and cemetery, and old, rambling walls. The Emperor's plans were
simple; he would contain Blücher's left and mount a crushing
assault which would drive in the Prussian centre. A heavy attack
on the Prussian right and centre would compel Blücher to commit
his reserves, and then, with the whole of the enemy engaged, Ney
would appear from Quatre Bras, taken, the Emperor imagined,
hours before, to envelop Blücher's right as the Imperial Guard
advanced through the *mêlée* to overwhelm the centre; two-thirds
of the army would be destroyed by Ney and the Guard, and the
remainder would retire in confusion on Liége.

At two, Napoleon instructed Soult to write to Ney. He stated
that the Emperor would attack the Prussians between Sombreffe
and Brye at half-past two; "His Majesty's intention is that you will
also attack whatever force is in front of you, and having vigorously
pushed it back, will turn in our direction, so as to bring about
the envelopment of the body of the enemy's troops I have just

* Wagnelée, La Haye, Petit Saint-Amand, Saint-Amand, Ligny, Potriaux,
Tongrinelle, Tongrinne, Boignée and Balâtre.

mentioned to you." Napoleon had high hopes of a decisive victory. "It is possible", he remarked to Gérard, "that three hours from now the fate of the war may be decided. If Ney executes his orders properly, not a single gun in this army will escape him." At two o'clock the Marshal was still south of Quatre Bras, discussing the forthcoming attack with Reille.

A little before three the battery of the Guard gave the signal for the battle to commence: three shots fired at regular intervals. Morale was excellent, confidence unbounded; Vandamme did not even bother to cannonade Saint-Amand before sending Lefol's division into the assault. Preceded by a swarm of skirmishers, the division advanced in three columns to the accompaniment of *La victoire en chantant*, played by the band of the 23rd Infantry Regiment. The Prussian artillery took heavy toll of the columns struggling through the four-foot high corn, and when the leading troops reached the village they were raked by volleys of point-blank musket fire. The French continued to advance in spite of their heavy losses, and within fifteen minutes they cleared the village of the enemy. The Prussian artillery turned their guns on the buildings in preparation for a counter-attack, and as the flames rose, the battle spread to the other villages along the Prussian front. Napoleon watched the beginning of the struggle, preoccupied by the need to bring Ney on to the field in good time.

At three-fifteen he decided to send a more explicit message than the last. "His Majesty desires me to tell you", wrote Soult,

> "that you are to manœuvre immediately to envelop the enemy's right and fall on his rear; the enemy on our front is lost if you act with energy. The fate of France is in your hands. Thus do not hesitate to carry out the manœuvre even for a moment . . . and direct your advance on the heights of Brye and Saint-Amand so as to co-operate in a victory that may well turn out to be decisive."

These instructions had scarcely been despatched when a message came from Lobau in Charleroi announcing that Ney was confronted by a force of 20,000 at Quatre Bras. Lobau had been left at Charleroi with the 6th Corps, and it is difficult to understand why Napoleon did not order these 10,000 men to join him when so vital a battle was to be fought. Had Lobau's corps left Charleroi at noon, it would have covered the eight miles to Fleurus by half-past three, and there would have been no need to rely on Ney to rout the Prussians. In the event, the 6th Corps was still four miles from the battlefield at half-past seven, and far too late to move against Blücher's right wing; "To leave Lobau at Charleroi", writes General Fuller, "was an inexcusable blunder."

Nevertheless, Lobau's despatch revealing the strength of Ney's opposition at Quatre Bras did not worry the Emperor very greatly. Reille's force should be sufficient to hold Wellington at the cross roads, leaving d'Erlon's corps free to march on the unsuspecting Blücher. D'Erlon's troops were still *en route* for Quatre Bras, and Napoleon sent off an aide-de-camp with a pencilled note to overtake the column and instruct it to march to his support, not Ney's. When the aide-de-camp had delivered his message, and turned d'Erlon's corps in the direction of the Prussians, he was to continue his journey and inform Ney of what had been done.

Meanwhile the battle for the villages continued with increasing violence. Clouds of smoke now covered long stretches of the Ligne, and from them emerged a continuous stream of wounded as fresh troops were marched into the struggle. The Prussians met attack with counter-attack, and the fighting became hand-to-hand in the constricted streets and outskirts of the villages. Blücher was obliged to send reinforcements to withstand the mounting pressure on his line, and the Emperor's plan was beginning to bear fruit.

At Quatre Bras Wellington's forces now slightly outnumbered the French, and Ney was still no nearer to capturing the road junction. A few minutes before four o'clock Soult's first letter arrived, announcing the Emperor's intention of attacking the Prussians and ordering him to press the enemy back and march against Blücher's right flank. This spurred Ney into ordering a general advance, but although ground was gained, the movement came to a halt without the capture of any important objective. Wellington's resistance was too strong to be overcome by the troops Ney had with him, and the Marshal decided to wait for d'Erlon's corps to arrive before attempting to seize the cross roads and comply with the Emperor's orders. The leading troops in d'Erlon's column were now quite close, and d'Erlon himself had galloped forward to reconnoitre their approaches to the battlefield. It was while he was away from his corps that Napoleon's aide caught up with the officers of d'Erlon's staff. Because the Emperor's pencilled handwriting was almost illegible, the aide-de-camp gave the wrong direction, and instead of telling d'Erlon's Chief of Staff to make for Saint-Amand, read the destination as Wagnelée. Within a few minutes the column had set off to join Napoleon.

D'Erlon returned from his reconnaissance to find his corps marching towards the Prussians, and he sent Delcambre, his Chief of Staff, back to Quatre Bras to inform Ney of the Emperor's orders. Ney's annoyance was great, for he was becoming increasingly outnumbered, and had counted on d'Erlon's assistance to win the battle. He had hardly received Delcambre's unwelcome news when Soult's second despatch arrived, declaring that "the Fate of France is in your hands". The exasperated Ney was still holding this letter when he noticed von Alten's division debouching from Quatre Bras. In an instant all sense of judgment was thrown to the winds; he did not stop to think that the need to crush the Prussian army far outweighed the importance of capturing Quatre Bras, and that in any case d'Erlon's corps was now too far away to be of any use to him that day. He sent Delcambre back to d'Erlon with an uncompromising order to return to Quatre Bras. D'Erlon was within sight of the battlefield of Ligny when Delcambre reached him, and his corps did not join Ney until after nightfall, having spent the day marching backwards and forwards between two battlefields. Ney must bear the chief responsibility for this fiasco, though d'Erlon should have disobeyed his last order on the grounds that a return to Quatre Bras could serve no useful purpose.

Ney was left with the problem of fighting Wellington without the help of d'Erlon's troops; and while his reinforcements were marching away from him, Wellington's continued to arrive. By now Ney had committed all the men he had with him, except for Kellermann's cuirassiers and the cavalry of the Guard. He resolved to strike a decisive blow with these last reserves. Kellermann was sent for and told that the safety of France was at stake; nothing short of an overwhelming attack could retrieve the situation. Kellerman was to take his cavalry, continued Ney, and charge the English infantry, trampling them underfoot. Ney could not have chosen a man less disposed to dispute an order to charge, but he was beside himself with anger, and Kellermann was not. The general pointed out that the English could not be far short of 25,000, and that three of his four brigades had been left several miles in the rear on Ney's own instructions. Ney was adamant. "Charge with what you have," he replied, "I will send after you all the cavalry I can muster." It was now Kellermann's turn to be blinded by emotion. Enraged that his courage should be questioned, and made desperate by the nature of the order, to charge the English lines with 900 men, he quickly formed his brigade into a column. "I used great haste", he wrote in his report after the battle, "so as not to allow my men time to shrink, or to see the whole extent of the danger in front of them." Kellermann gave the order to charge, and led the way himself, sword unsheathed, at full gallop, 20 yards in front of the leading squadrons.

This supreme effort, this heroic sacrifice, might have turned the day if it had been properly supported. But Kellermann had launched his troops too suddenly for assistance to reach him, and Ney was slow in supporting the charge; he had, moreover, completely forgotten the cavalry of the Guard lying idle near Frasnes.

The 69th Regiment, who occupied a valley to the south of the cross roads, were the first to meet the cuirassiers. Halkett, the brigade commander, had noticed the French cavalry form up for the attack, and sent the 69th the order to form squares. Another officer, on the spot, was unable to see the French, and once more instructed the regiment to deploy in line; the 69th were doing this as the cavalry came upon them. They preserved their ranks in silence and fired when the charging horsemen were thirty yards away. The impetus of the cuirassiers was so great that they swept through the smoke and bullets without stopping, scattered the ranks of the infantry and captured their colours. Beyond the debris of the 69th was the square of the 30th, which Kellermann's troops charged without breaking. Next they dislodged the 33rd, which had not had time to form properly. Having penetrated Wellington's first and second lines, the horsemen swept up the slope of the valley without pausing to reform, cut down the gunners of a battery, broke through a square of Brunswickers, and finally arrived at the cross roads of Quatre Bras itself. Here they paid the penalty of their success; greatly outnumbered, they lay in the centre of the English positions, whose fire poured in on them. No support was sent to distract the enemy and when Kellermann's horse was shot beneath him, the cuirassiers panicked. In vain Kellermann rose from the ground and attempted to rally his men. The system of command, always so difficult to preserve in a cavalry charge, collapsed as the survivors wheeled round, deaf to Kellermann's shouts, and spurred their horses through the disordered but vehement fire of the infantry they had passed on their way to the cross roads. They reached their own lines out of control, and dragged several battalions of infantry after them in their flight. Fresh cavalry were sent forward, but they could make no impression on the English squares without the support of their own infantry. Ney had hoped to make Kellermann's charge the preliminary to capturing Quatre Bras, but the sole result was that his hard-pressed line became weaker. The enemy began to exploit the French reverse, and Wellington was bringing up reinforcements to press the advantage home when Major Badus approached Ney with a verbal message from the Emperor.

Napoleon insisted that his orders to d'Erlon must be obeyed, whatever the circumstances at Quatre Bras. The fighting there was of small importance compared with the task of defeating the entire Prussian army. If Ney could do nothing more, he must be content with holding the English army to its present positions. Ney's face turned red with anger at this, and he flourished his sword in the air as he shouted at Badus. He ignored the Major's pleadings to countermand the order to d'Erlon, and breaking off the conversation abruptly, rushed into the middle of his disintegrating infantry, rallied them, and led them in a counter-attack.

It was Wellington's habit to advance only when sure of success, and although the French fought stubbornly to hold the ground they had won that afternoon, the numbers against them were too great to be withstood. The French began to fall back slowly until at nightfall the armies occupied the ground they had held at midday. Wellington had lost 4,700 killed and wounded and Ney 4,300.

Neither commander had distinguished himself; less than half Wellington's army had arrived by the end of the battle, and Ney who had known better than the Duke what was afoot, had concentrated only 22,000 of the 43,000 under his orders. Wellington's mistakes were not confined to his miscalculation and delay on the

15th, for he found himself at Quatre Bras with insufficient cavalry and artillery for the infantry that did arrive.

The task of housing and feeding the army had obliged the Duke to scatter his cantonments over a wide area, but there had been months in which to make sure that each detachment of infantry was established in the neighbourhood of enough guns and horsemen to constitute a balanced force. Yet when the fighting at Quatre Bras died down on the evening of the 16th Wellington had only a third of his artillery and a seventh of his cavalry. Sergeant Morris was keenly aware of this piece of carelessness. "Fortunately for the Duke", he concluded, "the result was successful; had it been otherwise, he would have been deeply censured."

Thanks to Ney's obstinacy Napoleon had been obliged to fight his battle at Ligny without d'Erlon's corps; nevertheless, he contrived to deliver a crippling blow to Blücher's army. For several hours after Soult's two messages to Ney the struggle had continued to ebb and flow in the villages along the Ligne. Many of the buildings were on fire, and the screams of the wounded trapped inside them added to the horrors of bitter hand-to-hand fighting and endless volleys of musketry across constricted spaces. Although most of his troops were under fire for the first time, Blücher's regiments fought stubbornly in these exceptional conditions, but they lacked the skill and courage of Napoleon's veteran army. By five Blücher had been obliged to commit his reserves, and the Imperial Guard remained intact behind the French lines waiting to assault the centre as Ney arrived on the Prussian right wing. Five o'clock came and went, and Napoleon grew increasingly impatient as the minutes passed without the sound of Ney's guns. The Emperor was still confident that it could not be long before the Prussians received their coup de grâce, when Vandamme galloped up from the left wing with the news that a strong enemy column was 3 miles away, marching on Fleurus and about to turn the French left. Both Ney and d'Erlon had been ordered to approach the battlefield by Saint-Amand and not Fleurus, but the Emperor was sure that the column was French. It was, of course, d'Erlon's corps, which was marching on Wagnelée, on the instructions of the aide-de-camp who had misread the pencilled destination given in the Emperor's note.

Vandamme was positive that they had to deal with a fresh enemy force; an officer had been sent to establish their identity, and he had galloped back to his commander shouting, "They are enemies, they are enemies!" Vandamme's aide was young and inexperienced, and had failed to go close enough to see which side they belonged to. Napoleon remained unconvinced, and sent one of his own aides-de-camp to examine the approaching force. As a precaution he suspended the attack of the Guard, which was now being prepared. Vandamme's corps abandoned La Haye in the belief that they were about to be attacked from the rear. Vandamme told Napoleon that he would be forced to withdraw from Saint-Amand as well unless the reserve were sent to support him. Some of the Guard were detached and hurried off to fill the gap.

The situation was becoming critical on the French left; at the sight of the column closing on their rear Lefol's division fled panic-stricken from their positions. Lefol turned his artillery on his men and obliged them to go back. Meanwhile, to take advantage of the confusion, Blücher ordered a heavy attack which the reinforcement from the Guard arrived in time to beat off. The turning-point had been reached. As the detachment of the Guard stemmed the Prussian advance, Girard's division advanced to capture Le Hameau for the third time that afternoon. Lefol and Berthézène rallied their troops and retook Saint-Amand. The battle continued vigorously along the whole front, but by now the Prussians lacked the men with whom to deliver a decisive assault.

Blücher was indefatigable in rallying stragglers and scattered formations, but they broke in his hands each time he led them to the attack, and he realised that his army had shot its bolt. Behind the French lines were the Imperial Guard, still untouched, and ready to march on Ligny. At last the Emperor was given confirmation that the mysterious column marching on Fleurus was French; it had in fact begun to disappear, though whether to outflank the Prussians or assist Ney in some desperate strait he could not tell. However, he could be sure that he would not be interrupted, and two hours later than he had intended, he ordered the Guard to attack. A tremendous cannonade burst out over Ligny and the Prussian centre.

Although it was only half-past seven, and sunset more than an hour away, the light was failing fast. Huge storm clouds had appeared over the battlefield, and peals of thunder began an accompaniment to the roar of the artillery. The storm burst as the infantry and cavalry of the Guard, shouting "*Vive l'Empereur!*" started their advance. The assault was pressed home through a downpour of warm rain; the priming pans of their muskets soaked, the dense mass of the Guard charged through Ligny without firing a shot. Behind them, to left and right, followed thousands of cavalry. The Prussian centre collapsed under the onslaught. "It was like a scene on the stage", Soult wrote to Davout. By the time Blücher had galloped from La Haye to the breach in his front the rain had stopped and the clouds had given way to the setting sun. The Field-Marshal had only two brigades of cavalry with which to stem the tide sweeping over his lines, and these he led against the Guard. The infantry formed squares, which beat off the repeated Prussian charges while the cuirassiers rode forward to counter-attack.

The struggle between the intermingled squadrons of the cavalry continued until nightfall, ebbing and flowing in front of the squares of the Guard which continued to advance slowly but inexorably up the slopes towards the mill at Bussy.

In one of the innumerable *mêlées* on the slopes Blücher's horse was hit by a musket ball and fell, pinning him to the ground. Nostiz, the Field-Marshal's aide-de-camp, dismounted to help him, and as he did so, a squadron of cuirassiers rode past in the dusk without noticing them. Minutes later the French fell back before a Prussian charge, again without discovering the injured commander. Nostiz called for help and the semi-conscious Blücher was dragged from beneath his horse and lifted into a subaltern's saddle to be led away to join the vast stream of fugitives making their escape in the shelter of the Prussian rearguard.

Napoleon had smashed the Prussian centre with complete success, but nightfall and the stubborn resistance of the two wings prevented him from turning a decisive defeat into a rout. The remains of the divisions which had defended the centre retreated in disorder to Sombreffe, while the cavalry held off their pursuers until darkness brought the French advance to a halt. The commanders on either wing did not begin their withdrawal until they were informed that

Ligny had fallen, and halted their forces just beyond Sombreffe. The Prussian rearguard held Brye itself till morning. Had d'Erlon's corps been at Sombreffe as the Prussians reeled back from the attack of the Guard, Blücher's army would have been scattered to the winds. It is even possible that the Guard could have accomplished almost as much by itself, if it had advanced as Napoleon had intended, two hours earlier. Nevertheless, Ligny had been a considerable victory for the French. Blücher's forces had to continue their retreat during the 17th, leaving Napoleon free to attack Wellington that day.

The Prussian losses in killed, wounded and captured cannot have been far short of 16,000, while those of the French were between 11,000 and 12,000. During the night at least a further 8,000 Prussians deserted the army and fled to Liége.*

As Blücher's divisions rallied around Sombreffe during the late evening, the Prussian corps commanders gathered at Brye where they expected to meet the Field-Marshal. His staff had no news of his whereabouts, for the dragoons who rescued Blücher from the battlefield had only just carried him to a cottage in the village of Mellery, and for all his staff knew he might well be dead or a prisoner. The command of the army devolved on Gneisenau, the senior general and Chief of Staff. Fearing to advance in darkness against an enemy capable of serious resistance and rumoured to have a reserve in the neighbourhood, Napoleon had called off the pursuit until daybreak, but Gneisenau could not afford to wait to see if Blücher should appear before deciding the Prussian line of retreat. Gneisenau was faced with the problem whether to withdraw away from Wellington along his lines of communication to Namur, or to adopt some other course. He studied his map for a few moments in the moonlight and decided to retreat on Wavre.

"This", Wellington wrote a few days later, "was the decisive moment of the century", but Gneisenau and his colleagues could have had no idea of that. The thought of marching from Wavre on the 18th to join the English at Waterloo never entered their heads, for they did not know whether Wellington meant to cover Brussels as he retreated from Quatre Bras. Wavre might well have

* These appear to have been recruited from provinces formerly part of the Empire and their loyalty was doubtful.

been too far from Wellington's withdrawal for any kind of co-operation, and Gneisenau's choice of the town is explained solely by its convenience as a rallying point and the ease with which the Prussians could defend themselves behind the stream on which it stood. From Wavre they would be able to continue their march to meet a variety of contingencies, among them a junction with Wellington's army. Thus Blücher's divisions were ordered to set off for Wavre early next morning. The conference at an end, Gneisenau made his way to Mellery, where he found Blücher lying on a bed of straw sipping a few mouthfuls of milk as he recovered from the effects of his fall.

5

The Seventeenth of June

THE MORNING OF SATURDAY the 17th of June was fine. In Brussels, Miss Charlotte Eaton was too uneasy to stay long in her bed. Below her windows the wounded and refugees from Quatre Bras now passed in a steady stream. "I again got up", she wrote in her diary,

> "a little after four o'clock. What a different sight from the morning before! An uninterrupted chain of carts going helter-skelter—cars with wounded soldiers—Belgian regiments seeming to be without any discipline or control—all pouring into the town; wounded soldiers lying on the pavement, having got as far as the town, but unable to crawl further—the dismay was universal."

Two hours later the Emperor rose at Fleurus and proceeded to breakfast. He was still at table when an aide-de-camp returned from Quatre Bras with the first news of Ney's doings on the 16th, for the Marshal had not previously bothered to send a despatch to Napoleon. Shortly afterwards a message timed 4 a.m. was received from Pajol, the commander of the cavalry following the Prussian withdrawal.

Pajol reported the Prussians to be in full retreat on Liége and Namur; this was the first of the day's misunderstandings, for the troops he had seen were the thousands of deserters who abandoned the army after the battle of Ligny; the main body of Blücher's army was about to march in a totally different direction, to Wavre. This mistake might have been quickly corrected, had Napoleon been prompt to send out more cavalry to cover the Prussian retreat, but when Grouchy arrived in search of fresh orders the Emperor told him to wait; he was to accompany Napoleon on a visit to the battlefield, where the army had spent the night, and he would be given his instructions there.

It was quite uncharacteristic of the Emperor to be so casual on the morrow of a victory; normally he would have issued orders to pursue the Prussians in force as soon as he rose, and would have made sure that Grouchy did so. Instead he spent most of the morning on the battlefield at Ligny, inspecting the troops, visiting the wounded, and discussing the political scene in Paris with his generals. Not until eleven did he set about securing the initiative he had won over Wellington and Blücher.

His historians have been impatient at this extraordinary delay, and endless reasons have been advanced for it. The more charitable writers suggest that Napoleon was waiting for further information before giving his orders to the army, but this scarcely makes sense because he knew at breakfast time that Wellington's army was still at Quatre Bras that morning, and yet not until four hours afterwards, when it was too late, did he think of seizing the opportunity to attack it there. He had not failed to issue orders promptly, but nothing constructive was set in hand until an hour before noon.

Another school of thought, which suggests that the Emperor was suffering from lack of sleep, stands on stronger ground, for Napoleon's early orders all bear the mark of a mind struggling against fatigue, glimmering very fitfully, ignoring information which ordinarily would have been sufficient to bring a lightning blow against his opponent. Grouchy's account of the morning gives weight to this argument, since he relates how, when he and the Emperor set out before nine o'clock for the battlefield, Napoleon's carriage jolted so violently over the furrows that, *tired as he was*, the Emperor got out and mounted a horse. Seven hours sleep on the previous night had not compensated for the long hours spent on horseback since before dawn on the 15th.

Before he left Fleurus, the Emperor dictated to Soult a curious set of instructions for Ney. He informed him of the result of the battle of Ligny, and went on to say:

> "The Emperor is going to the mill of Brye, where the highway from Namur to Quatre Bras passes. This makes it impossible that the English Army should act in front of you. In the latter event, the Emperor would march directly on it by the Quatre

Bras road, while you would attack it from the front, and this
army would be destroyed in an instant. Therefore keep His
Majesty informed of whatever takes place in front of you. . . .
His Majesty's wishes are that you should take up your position
at Quatre Bras; but if this is impossible, and cannot be accomplished, send information immediately with full details, and the
Emperor will act there as I have told you. If, on the contrary,
there is only a rearguard, attack it and seize the position.
Today it is absolutely necessary to end this operation, and
complete the military stores, to rally scattered soldiers and
summon back all detachments.''

There are few stranger documents in Napoleon's vast campaign
correspondence, and for this Soult may be largely to blame; he
had never previously served as Chief of Staff, and it is not surprising
that his despatches are so much less clear than Berthier's whose
experience and skill had served the Emperor from the time of his
first campaign in Italy in 1796.

Nevertheless the message to Ney is so obscure that it must be
presumed that the Emperor's own mind was not clear early that
morning. It suggests that Napoleon thought it likely that Wellington was withdrawing the bulk of his forces from Quatre Bras,
leaving only a rearguard. On the other hand, he could not be sure,
and should the English still be there, he would swing over sufficient
troops from Ligny to enable Ney to drive Wellington back. The
last sentence infers that the Emperor was almost sure that the
English were retreating. If this was his view the mystery only
thickens, for a leisurely consolidation following the previous day's
operations was the last thing to be thinking of immediately after a
resounding victory over the Prussians. The despatch to Ney is so
thoroughly muddled that it can be made to mean almost anything,
and therefore nothing. What is sure, however, is that normally
at 7 a.m. Napoleon would have given Ney the instructions he
issued at eleven. The obvious thing to do, as he saw later, was to
exploit the severing of the allied front as quickly as possible. A
strong detachment would be sufficient to see that the Prussians
continued to retreat away from Wellington while the mass of the
army overwhelmed the English. Prompt action would bring
Wellington to battle as he retreated, for Ney's early despatch
reported the English to be at Quatre Bras in force at first light. The
Emperor's failure to send off two corps to Quatre Bras before nine

that morning cannot have been because he did not know what was going on, but because his mind was not yet functioning with its usual lucidity. Had he thought clearly as he dressed and breakfasted it would have occurred to him that if he had received no news from Ney about the previous day's happenings at Quatre Bras, it was even less likely that Wellington had learnt anything from Blücher, especially as his ally had suffered a serious defeat. Wellington was almost sure to remain where he was until news of the Prussian reverse reached him, for his strength lay in operating in concert with Blücher, and with the whole of his army around him, he would not be frightened away by Ney's smaller force.

That was exactly what had happened; Wellington did not hear of Blücher's defeat until half-past seven, and the news was as much a surprise to him as it was to his officers: "Previous to the receipt of Blücher's despatches", writes an English officer,

"we were all in high spirits, anticipating a splendid victory over the French marshal before night—never doubting but Blücher would be able to keep Bonaparte at bay, whilst we, having the whole of our army united, amused ourselves with Ney. But the moment that the retreat of Blücher was made known, our spirits were as much depressed as they had been elated before. A gloom spread over the countenances of us all. Every soldier was more or less affected. . . . For some time after he had received the unwelcome news, his Grace remained closely shut up in the hut. Having issued the necessary orders for the retreat of the army, he came out of his airy residence, and for an hour walked alone in front of it. Now and then his meditations were interrupted by a courier with a note, who, the moment he had delivered it, retired to some distance to wait his General's will. The Field-Marshal had a small switch in his right hand, the one end of which he frequently put in his mouth, apparently unconscious that he was doing so. His left hand was thrown behind his back, and he walked at the rate of three and a half to four miles in the hour. He was dressed in white pantaloons, with half-boots, a military vest, white neckcloth, blue surtout and cocked hat."

The situation at Quatre Bras continued to preoccupy the Emperor after the first despatch to Ney had gone, and at half-past eight, before he went to his coach, he ordered a cavalry reconnaissance of Wellington's positions. He also decided to send an infantry division to support Pajol on the road to Namur, where the Count's cavalry were following or so they thought, the Prussian retreat.

Some minutes before nine o'clock he climbed into his coach to ride to Ligny.

The Emperor's instructions reached Ney shortly after nine, but he took no steps to execute them, so that for the next four hours Wellington was allowed to retreat without any interference from the French. When Napoleon arrived on the scene at two the only excuse Ney had to offer for his inactivity was that he thought that he had the whole of the English army before him. As the Emperor remarked at St. Helena, Ney was no longer the man he used to be. He had not even bothered to send out a patrol to discover what the English were doing. Napoleon learnt of Wellington's retreat not from Ney, whose troops faced the English army, but from the cavalry he had ordered to reconnoitre Quatre Bras before he left Fleurus that morning. Left to himself by Ney, Wellington had been able to begin his retreat in peace. At half-past seven his first reaction to Blücher's despatch was to withdraw at once. "Old Blücher has had a damned good licking and gone back to Wavre, eighteen miles. As he has gone back, we must go too. I suppose in England they will say we have been licked; well, I can't help it; as they are gone back, we must go too."

Müffling, the Prussian commissioner attached to the Duke's staff, argued that there was no reason to abandon all hope of co-operating with Blücher. He was equally sure that there was no need for a hurried retreat; the French remained quiet and were not likely to move before they had cooked themselves a meal. The Duke gave orders for the army to begin the withdrawal at ten, and in the meantime troops who were still *en route* for Quatre Bras would march instead to Waterloo, a village in the rear of a strong defensive position he had reconnoitred some months before, and which he had pointed out to the Duke of Richmond as a suitable place to make a stand against Napoleon. "Having satisfied himself that the enemy were still quiet", writes Sir Hussey Vivian, one of Wellington's cavalry commanders,

> "he then lay himself down on the ground, covered his head with one of the newspapers he had been reading, and appeared to fall asleep, and in this way he remained some time; when he again arose and mounted his horse and rode down the field in front of Quatre Bras a little distance, and looked about through his glass, and I perfectly well remember his expressing

his astonishment at the perfect quiet of the enemy and his saying
that it was 'not at all impossible that they were retreating'."

A Prussian aide came up with the news that the whole of Blücher's
army was retreating on Wavre, and asked the Duke for details
of the English movements. He told the aide-de-camp to inform
his commander that he would take up a position at Mont-Saint-
Jean, the ridge to the south of the village of Waterloo, wait for
Napoleon and fight him there, provided he could count on the
assistance of one Prussian corps. Without this support, said Wellington, he would be forced to abandon Brussels and establish a line
behind the Scheldt. Shortly after the Prussian officer's departure,
the English began to withdraw. Three hours went by, until only
the English cavalry and horse artillery remained at the cross roads.
Mercer's battery was one of those which stayed with the rearguard, and Lord Uxbridge, the commander of the cavalry, and his
aide-de-camp sat down with him in front of his guns.

> "His Lordship with his glass was watching the French
> position; and we were all three wondering at their want of
> observation and inactivity, which had not only permitted our
> infantry to retire unmolested, but also still retained them in their
> bivouac. 'It will not be long now before they are on us', said
> the aide-de-camp, 'for they always dine before they move;
> and those smokes seem to indicate that they are cooking now.'"

The first French troops to arrive on the scene, however, were not
Ney's, but the Emperor's.

Accompanied by Grouchy, Napoleon reached the French lines
around Ligny a little before ten. On the way there Grouchy ventured to ask again for instructions, only to be snubbed for his
pains; "I will give you them when I see fit", said the Emperor.
More than an hour was spent inspecting the wounded lying on
the field, congratulating the troops and discussing public opinion
in Paris with Grouchy and a number of generals. Napoleon's
commanders were becoming alarmed at his indifference to the
need to pursue the allied armies, but when fresh despatches were
received at eleven, he suddenly awoke from his trance and set to
work with all his accustomed skill and energy. Lobau was sent
off with the 6th Corps to take the English left flank at Quatre
Bras, Drouot and the whole of the Imperial Guard were to follow
him. Grouchy was at last given his orders; he was to pursue the

Prussians while the bulk of the army joined the Emperor to march on Wellington. The latest reports suggested that Blücher's army was continuing to march on Namur, and Grouchy was to begin by looking for them in that direction. He had not long been gone before Napoleon sent written instructions after him. His force was to be concentrated at Gembloux, a convenient centre from which to reconnoitre Namur, Liége and Wavre. He was to discover the whereabouts of the Prussians and establish whether Blücher intended to bring his army to Wellington's support. Quite needlessly, the Prussians had been allowed to slip away unmolested, and for the time being at least, the Emperor had lost all knowledge of Blücher's movements and therefore his probable intentions; it was a formidable price to pay for a few hours' lethargy. As long as Blücher evaded Grouchy's cavalry the Emperor would endanger himself by attempting to fight the English, for should Blücher reach Wellington before the English were defeated, Napoleon had lost the campaign. The Emperor was convinced that the Prussians had taken such punishment at Ligny that their army would not soon be ready for further fighting, and even if they were, Grouchy should be able to prevent a junction of the allied armies until Wellington had been settled with.

The Marshal had only to keep in contact with Blücher's forces and be ready to place himself in the path of any attempt to attack Napoleon while the French were engaged with Wellington. Unfortunately for Napoleon, the Prussians were able to fight again within thirty-six hours, and Grouchy did not make the best of his critical position; he had been reluctant to assume independent command, for it was his first experience of such a rôle, and he knew that his subordinates had little confidence in him. Next day his ruin was complete, and for this some of the responsibility was Napoleon's.

By twelve the Emperor had completed his arrangements for the Prussians, and hurried off westwards to see what could be made of the situation at Quatre Bras. There was good reason to hope that Wellington might already be brought to bay, for by now Ney's troops should be at grips with the English; and the arrival of the Emperor's troops should ensure complete victory. At the very least, Ney's force should be ready to join him in pursuing the

English and bringing them to battle. Napoleon neared Quatre Bras a little after two, and to his astonishment, could see none of Ney's men, though large numbers of Wellington's cavalry were about. He sent messengers to hasten the arrival of Ney's corps commanders and their troops, and while he waited impatiently for them to join him, he examined the English rearguard.

Dark clouds had gathered over the slopes on which they stood, and the morning's sultry heat was about to give way to a torrential downpour. The storm had reached Brussels an hour before. "About one o'clock", wrote Miss Charlotte Eaton,

> "the most dreadful storm of thunder and lightning I ever recollect came on. We were obliged to shut the shutters. . . . Lord Apsley came to me with a message from the Duke of Wellington to say that he had been obliged to retreat to the last position before he gave up Brussels; that he hoped to be able to retain it, but as it was very uncertain, he advised us to have horses quite ready, and all our things packed up. . . . During the whole evening and night the rain fell in torrents. I do not remember for a continuance of so many hours having ever seen it so heavy; it was exactly as if pitchers of water were pouring down."

Napoleon could now see how great a chance he as well as Ney had let slip that morning; had he ordered his troops to march at eight instead of eleven, Wellington would have been forced to fight at Quatre Bras against such superior numbers that for all intents and purposes, the campaign would have been over by the evening. Like Blücher, he had been given a few hours' grace, and with it he might be able to evade defeat. At last d'Erlon joined the Emperor with his corps. "France has been ruined!" Napoleon exclaimed to him; "Go, my dear General, place yourself at the head of the cavalry and press the English rearguard vigorously." When Ney came up the Emperor was too busy organising the pursuit to waste time in reproaches, and said merely that he was surprised that his orders for the occupation of Quatre Bras had not been carried out. The Marshal's sole excuse for not stirring all morning was that he thought that he had the whole of Wellington's army before him, which was, of course, no excuse at all. Giving rapid instructions to Ney that the rest of the army should follow him as quickly as possible, and taking a battery of horse artillery and the *escadrons de service*, Napoleon galloped to the head of the column to spur the pursuit.

That afternoon, his last in open campaign, was worthy of the general of Italy and Austerlitz; he led the vanguard with all his former energy and determination, and had the weather held he must have caught up with Wellington before nightfall. "One ought to have been witness of ... a march more like a steeplechase than the pursuit of a retreating enemy", wrote an officer who accompanied the Emperor,

> "to realise the energy Napoleon knew how to inspire in the troops under his immediate command.... The Emperor, mounted on a small and very active horse, galloped at the head of the column; he was constantly close to the guns, stimulating the gunners by his presence and words, and more than once he was in the thick of the shells and balls which the English poured on us."

Captain Mercer was waiting by his guns at the top of the slopes when he first caught sight of Napoleon:

> "There was a degree of sublimity in the interview rarely equalled. The sky had become overcast since the morning, and at this moment presented a most extraordinary appearance. Large isolated masses of thundercloud, of the deepest, almost inky black ... hung over us, involving our position and everything in it in deep and gloomy obscurity; whilst the distant hill lately occupied by the French army still lay bathed in brilliant sunshine. Lord Uxbridge was yet speaking, when a single horseman [Napoleon] immediately followed by several others, mounted the plateau I had left at a gallop, their dark figures thrown forward in strong relief from the illuminated distance, making them appear much nearer to us than they really were. For an instant they pulled up and regarded us, when several squadrons, coming rapidly on the plateau, Lord Uxbridge cried out 'Fire!—fire!' and giving them a general discharge, we quickly limbered up to retire, as they dashed forward supported by some horse artillery guns.... The first gun that was fired seemed to burst the clouds overhead, for its report was instantly followed by an awful clap of thunder, and lightning that almost blinded us, whilst the rain came down as if a water-spout had broken over us. The sublimity of the scene was inconceivable. Flash followed flash, and the peals of thunder were long and tremendous; whilst, as if in mockery of the elements, the French guns still sent forth their feebler glare and now scarcely audible reports—their cavalry dashing on at a headlong pace, adding their shouts to the uproar. We galloped

for our lives through the storm, striving to gain the enclosures about the houses of the hamlets, Lord Uxbridge urging us on, crying, 'Make haste!—make haste! for God's sake gallop, or you will be taken!'"

The English beat a skilful retreat before the enemy. The artillery paused to fire at every opportunity, and the cavalry launched brief counter-attacks whenever the leading French squadrons became too daring. Many of Wellington's horsemen were inexperienced, but a veteran of the Peninsular War who watched the Life Guards praised their determination as well as laughing at a survival of peace-time habits:

"They had no idea of anything but straightforward fighting, and sent their opponents flying in all directions. The only young thing they showed was in everyone who got a roll in the mud (and owing to the slipperiness of the ground, there were many) going off to the rear, according to their Hyde Park custom, as being no longer fit to appear on parade. I thought at first that they had all been wounded, but, on finding how the case stood, I could not help telling them that theirs was now to verify the old proverb, 'The uglier the better soldier!'"

The Emperor's chase began two hours too late, but he led it at such a headlong pace that had the weather been normal he would probably have broken through Wellington's rearguard and caught up with the body of the army before it was safely established in the Waterloo position. The bulk of his troops would have been too far behind for a major engagement to be fought, but at least he would have had an opportunity of striking a damaging blow at Wellington's force. The heavy rain, however, robbed the French of their superior mobility, and instead of advancing across country in open order, as they were accustomed to, they were obliged to use the single crowded road, for the fields on either side were so water-logged that their horses sank half-way to their knees. "It became impossible for the French cavalry to press our columns in any force", wrote one of the English rearguard. "In fact, out of the road in the track of our own cavalry the ground was poached into a complete puddle."

Mercer's battery reached Genappe with the enemy close behind them, and rode through the lines of the Life Guards drawn up along the ridge outside the town. Behind them a cavalry skirmish broke out in the streets they had just left, and given this respite

99

Mercer unlimbered his guns. The pursuit slowed to a standstill as both sides engaged their cavalry and artillery. Presently Mercer ran short of ammunition, and he suggested to his superiors that the rockets should be used to conceal the shortage. Major McDonald argued that the range was too far, and Mercer proposed he shortened it by marching nearer to the skirmishers in the town below. Having made the suggestion, he felt obliged to join the Rocket Troop. The rockets did not delay the French for long, for after a lucky hit at the outset, the rest went astray, and when the French artillerymen returned to their guns, Mercer and the rocketeers were obliged to beat a retreat back to the ridge and their empty ammunition cases. "As we had overtaken the rear of our infantry", wrote Mercer,

"it became necessary to make a stand here to enable them to gain ground. Major McDonald therefore sent me in pursuit of my ammunition-waggons, since all in our limbers was expended. . . . The ammunition-waggons I found coming up, and was returning with them when I met my whole troop again retiring by the road, whilst the cavalry did so by alternate regiments across the fields. The ground offering no feature for another stand, we continued thus along the road. The infantry had made so little progress that we again overtook the rear of their column, composed of Brunswickers. . . . These poor lads were pushing on at a great rate. As soon as their rear divisions heard the sound of our horses' feet, without once looking behind them, they began to crowd and press on those in front, until at last, hearing us close up to them, and finding it impossible to push forward in the road, many of them broke off into the fields; and such was their panic that, in order to run lighter, away went arms and knapsacks in all directions, and a general race ensued, the whole corps being in the most horrid confusion. It was to no purpose that I exerted my little stock of German to make them understand that we were their English friends. . . . We, however, still kept on our way, and soon after passed a few houses by the roadside, which I after-wards found was La Belle Alliance. Hence we crossed another valley, and on rising the opposite hill I found a capital position on the top of an old gravel-pit, which I occupied without loss of time. Behind the ground on which my guns were formed was a long hedge . . . which prevented our seeing anything beyond; as no troops were in sight except those following us across the valley, we had then no idea that we had arrived in the position where our whole army was assembled. . . .

"We did not long remain idle, for the guns were scarcely loaded ere the rear of our cavalry came crowding upon the

infantry corps we had passed, and which were then only crossing the valley, the French advance skirmishing with these,
whilst their squadrons occupied the heights. We waited a
little until some of their larger masses were assembled, and
then opened our fire with a range across the valley of about
1200 yards. The echo of our first gun had not ceased, when,
to my astonishment, a heavy cannonade, commencing in a most
startling manner from behind our hedge, rolled along the rising
ground, on part of which we were posted. The truth now
flashed on me; we had rejoined the army, and it is impossible
to describe the pleasing sense of security I felt at now having
the support of something more staunch than cavalry."

It was now nearly half-past six, and for a while the rain had
ceased to fall. Standing at the edge of the plateau of Mont Saint-
Jean, Mercer caught his second glimpse of the Emperor as he
arrived at La Belle Alliance surrounded by a large retinue. Some
of Mercer's men turned their guns on the French staff; one shot,
"pointed by old Quartermaster Hall, fell into the middle of them.
At the moment we saw some little confusion amongst the group,
but it did not hinder them from continuing the reconnaissance."
Napoleon was anxious to discover whether the whole of the
English army lay before him across the misty valley or whether
Wellington had merely left a strong rearguard to cover his continued retreat. Four field batteries were ordered to fire at the
English while a detachment of cuirassiers charged up the slope to
the enemy's lines. The English artillery fire was redoubled, the
horsemen returned: the whole of Wellington's army was there.
Reassured that his opponent had halted, the Emperor ordered his
artillery to cease fire; the enemy rapidly followed suit.

"Fancy yourself", wrote Lieutenant Hope in a letter home,

> "seated on a few small twigs, or a little straw, in a newly
> ploughed field, well soaked with six hours heavy rain;—your
> feet six or eight inches deep in the mud;—a thin blanket your
> only shelter . . .—cold, wet, and hungry, without a fire, with-
> out meat, and without drink.—Imagine yourself placed in such
> a situation and you will have a faint idea of what we suffered
> on the night of the 17th and the morning of the memorable
> 18th of June."

Wretched though the condition of the allied army was, the
French were still worse off. Most of the infantry had still a long way
to march before they could bivouac; they continued to arrive in

the French lines until after midnight, and those who came after nightfall had little chance to make themselves comfortable. Across the valley only the cavalry who had served as rearguard took up their positions after dark. On both sides there was little shelter, little food and little sleep. "Being close to the enemy", Sergeant Wheeler of the 51st Light Infantry wrote home shortly after the battle,

> "we could not use our blankets, the ground was too wet to lie down, we sat on our knapsacks until daylight without fires, there was no shelter against the weather; the water ran in streams from the cuffs of our Jackets, in short we were as wet as if we had been plunged over head in a river. We had one consolation, we knew the enemy were in the same plight.
>
> "The morning of the 18th June broke upon us and found us drenched with rain, benumbed and shaking with the cold. We stood to our arms and moved to a fresh spot to get out of the mud. You often blamed me for smoking when I was at home last year, but I must tell you if I had not had a good stock of tobacco this night I must have given up the Ghost."

Young Ensign Leeke, of the 52nd Foot, seventeen years old and only six weeks in the army, snatched a little sleep, possibly from sheer exhaustion.

> "My friend Yonge shared my boatcloak and straw with me, and we consequently both of us got very wet. The horses were picketed near us, and very soon some half-dozen of them got loose and galloped away towards Hougoumont and the French position, and then came back again at speed towards the horses they had left, nearly passing over us, and only being prevented from doing so by our jumping up; they galloped about in this way the whole night, and thus made this wretched night still more wretched. I fell asleep several times, then dreamt we were advancing and closing with the enemy, then started up again, then thought of home and all my beloved ones there; again I dozed off, then came our horses like a furious charge of cavalry, and we had to start up and scare them off."

Mercer and his friends set up a small tent, but the rain was too heavy even for the most seasoned campaigners to keep themselves dry.

> "Rolling ourselves in our wet blankets, (we) huddled close together, in hope, wet as we were, and wet as the ground was, of keeping each other warm. I knew not how my bedfellows got on, as we all lay for a long while perfectly still and silent— the old Peninsular hands disdaining to complain before their

18 *Wellington*

Detail from the portrait by Sir Thomas Lawrence

19 *Blücher*

From a contemporary engraving

Johnny Newcome comrades, and these fearing to do so lest they should provoke some such remarks as 'Lord have mercy on your poor tender carcass! what would such as you have done in the Pyrenees?' or 'Oho my boy! this is but child's play to what *we* saw in Spain.' So all who did not sleep (I believe the majority) pretended to do so, and bore their suffering with admirable heroism. For my part I once or twice, from sheer fatigue, got into something like a doze; yet it would not do. There was no possibility of sleeping, for besides being already so wet, the tent proved no shelter, the water pouring through the canvas in streams; so up I got, and to my infinite joy, found that some of the men had managed to make a couple of fires, round which they were sitting smoking their short pipes in something like comfort. The hint was a good one, and at that moment, my second captain joining me, we borrowed from them a few sticks, and choosing the best spot under the hedge, proceeded to make a fire for ourselves. In a short time we succeeded in raising a cheerful blaze, which materially bettered our situation. My companion had an umbrella (which, by the way, had afforded some merriment to our people on the march);* this we planted against the sloping bank of the hedge, and seating ourselves under it, he on one side of the stick, me on the other, we lighted cigars and became—comfortable."

There was more to endure than the cold and the wet; the supply waggons had failed to keep up with the armies and the troops had finished the rations with which they had been issued at the beginning of the campaign. Unless they had been able to buy or loot fresh supplies they were now desperately hungry. Some had scarcely anything to eat on the 17th and fought throughout the 18th on empty stomachs. Their first thought at the end of the day was to find water and then something to eat. Mercer ate nothing on the 17th until late at night. He and his second captain were sitting by

* The Duke, who was indifferent to the way his officers chose to dress, drew the line at umbrellas. "At Bayonne, in December, 1813", writes Captain Gronow, "His Grace, on looking round, saw to his surprise, a great many umbrellas, with which the officers protected themselves from the rain that was then falling, Arthur Hill came galloping up to us saying, 'Lord Wellington does not approve of the use of umbrellas during the enemy's firing, and will not allow the "gentlemen's sons" to make themselves ridiculous in the eyes of the army.' Colonel Tynling, a few days afterwards, received a wigging from Lord Wellington for suffering his officers to carry umbrellas in the face of the enemy; His Lordship observing, 'The Guards may in uniform, when on duty at St. James' carry them if they please, but in the field it is not only ridiculous but unmilitary.'" Mercer's Battery Surgeon carried one under fire at Waterloo.

the fire they had made when a passing Hanoverian asked permission to warm himself. After a while he got up to go, and

> "what was our surprise when, after fumbling in his haversack for some time, he pulled out a poor half-starved chicken, presented it to us and marched off. This was a god-send, in good truth, to people famished as we were; so calling for a camp-kettle, our prize was on the fire in a twinkling. Our comrades in the tent did not sleep so soundly but that they heard what was going on, and the kettle was hardly on the fire ere my gentlemen were assembled round it, a wet and shivering group, but all eager to partake of our good fortune—and so eager that, after various betrayals of impatience, the miserable chicken was at last snatched from the kettle ere it was half-boiled, pulled to pieces, and speedily devoured. I got a leg for my share, but it was not one mouthful, and this was the only food I tasted since the night before."

Wellington had established his headquarters at an inn in the small village of Waterloo on the Brussels-Charleroi road, 3 miles north of the English lines. Here he awaited a message from Blücher, for he intended to retreat that night unless he was promised the support of a Prussian corps. As the hours passed without news from his ally his situation grew increasingly dangerous; before long it would be too late to issue orders to withdraw, and he had soon to decide whether or not to risk the chance of Blücher's coming to his assistance. At last, at 2 a.m., a letter arrived from the Prussian commander: "Bülow's corps", it read, "will set off marching in your direction at daybreak tomorrow. It will be followed immediately by Pirch's corps. The 1st and 2nd Corps will also be ready to proceed towards you. The exhaustion of the troops, part of which have not yet arrived, does not allow my commencing my movement earlier." These reinforcements were far more than the Duke had hoped for, and he determined to offer battle next morning.

The Emperor's headquarters were set up at Le Caillou, a farm a mile and a half to the south of La Belle Alliance. At nine o'clock that evening, soon after his arrival, one of Napoleon's officers reported that a patrol had sighted a Prussian column marching on Wavre. The Emperor, quite convinced that even if Blücher's army were in a condition to fight, he would not dare to march across the French flank to join Wellington when Grouchy was following him with over 30,000 men, dismissed this invaluable information as being a piece of misinterpretation. Before he went to bed Napoleon dictated the order of battle for the next day, so that an early start might be possible, and then several letters to Paris, where the uneasy political situation continued to occupy his attention. The Emperor did not rest for long, for by one he was up again, and went out with Bertrand to make a round of the outposts through the pouring rain. He returned at dawn assured that Wellington had decided to hold his ground.

An hour after he had left to make his tour of inspection a despatch was received at Le Caillou from Grouchy, timed Gembloux, 2 p.m. Grouchy had pursued the Prussians so slowly that when he halted his forces for the night he had gone no farther than Gembloux. Nevertheless, the information he had gathered, together with the report of a Prussian column marching on Wavre, should have convinced the officers at Le Caillou that Blücher would attempt to intervene in the battle for Mont-Saint-Jean. Blücher's army appeared to be withdrawing in two directions, the despatch stated, one towards Wavre and the other towards Perwez. "Perhaps it may be inferred that one portion is going to join Wellington, whilst the centre, under Blücher, retires on Liége; another column, accompanied by guns, had already retreated to Namur. . . . If I find that the mass of the Prussian army is retiring on Wavre I shall follow them, so as to prevent their gaining Brussels and to separate them from Wellington." The only answer Napoleon's staff saw fit to send to this message was a duplicate of routine orders issued some hours before.

This was rather less than the situation deserved; Grouchy should have been instructed that a battle was to be fought at Mont-Saint-Jean, and that he should at once move closer to the rest of the army in order to make sure that the allies did not join forces. If this had been done by 8 a.m. at the latest, Grouchy would have known what to do and the danger of a crushing Prussian intervention would have been avoided. Although Grouchy's proposals seemed to provide for the possibility of Blücher trying to reach Wellington, he could not know how essential it was to hold the allies apart when he had not been told that the Emperor would be already engaged with the English by the time Blücher would appear.

At first sight Napoleon's staff are to blame for this oversight, but in fact the Emperor himself was far more culpable, for when he returned at dawn and was shown Grouchy's despatch, he thought so little of its importance that he did not reply to it until 10 a.m., an hour before the battle began. Grouchy was left to infer for himself that morning what the sound of cannon-fire to the west should mean. His generals argued that they should march on the guns, but he insisted that he had the Emperor's orders to obey, and this he did, in an unimaginative fashion. No doubt an abler or a more experienced commander would have written his own orders when he realised that a major battle was being fought 12 miles away, and that unless he was prompt, the army in whose rear he was marching might wheel to join the enemy at Mont-Saint-Jean before he could stop them. Yet any blame that rests on Grouchy rests tenfold on Napoleon, who was certainly more able and experienced and who remained just as blind to the danger-ousness of his situation. At dawn the Emperor should have instructed his subordinate to head the Prussians off from Welling-ton by marching at once towards Mont-Saint-Jean and placing himself where Blücher would debouch on to the field. Had this been done the battle of Waterloo would have been won and Grouchy would not have been cast as the scapegoat for Napoleon's defeat.

Grouchy's conduct of his command is open to a good deal of justifiable criticism, though none of it so damning as some of the charges which have been levelled against him. He should have set his troops in motion by dawn on the 18th, that is, by 3.30, for whether or not there was to be a battle between the Emperor and the English, his task was to keep the Prussians away from Welling-ton and Brussels, and the longer he delayed in resuming his pursuit, the farther he would be in their rear and the less he would be capable of influencing their march.

Instead of enforcing an early start, he allowed his corps to move off between eight and nine that morning. This heavy disadvantage might still have been partly redeemed if he had chosen a more sensible route than the one he gave his forces. He should have left Blücher's rear-guard to its own devices, and have marched along the flank of the Prussian army. In the event he followed in their trail, and became so entangled with a single corps that the rest were able to journey almost unmolested to Wellington's assistance. Yet grave though these mistakes were, they do not outweigh the Emperor's error in not summoning Grouchy to his side at dawn on the 18th in terms which left him in no doubt of the urgency of the situation; instead, Grouchy did not receive Napoleon's 10 a.m. despatch until 4 p.m. The Emperor failed to send for Grouchy, because, despite a growing body of evidence, he refused to believe that Blücher would join the English.

6

Waterloo: Morning

WHEN DAWN BROKE ON SUNDAY, the 18th of June, it brought no respite from the rain which had now been falling for many hours. The bedraggled figures which rose from the sodden ground were not the resplendent heroes of popular imagination; they were cold, wet and hungry, and their beards were three and four days old. The officers of the Scots Greys were covered in mud from head to foot, and the dye of their red jackets had run over their white belts, "as if", said one of them, "we had already completed the sanguinary work we were about to begin". "The sun . . . broke but slowly through the heavy clouds", wrote Sergeant-Major Cotton.

> "The rain descended in torrents, succeeded, as the morning advanced, by a drizzling shower which gradually ceased. Soon after the break of day, all who were able were on the move. Many, from cold and fatigue, could not stir for some time; fortunately, on most of us the excitement was too powerful to allow this physical inconvenience to be much felt. . . . Some were cleaning arms, others fetching wood, water, straw, etc., from Mont-Saint-Jean. . . . Some trying, from the embers of our bivac, to light up fires, many of which had been entirely put out by the heavy rain. At this time there was a continual irregular popping along the line, not unlike a skirmish, occasioned by those who were cleaning their firearms, discharging them when practicable; which was more expeditious and satisfactory than drawing the charges. Our bivac had a most unsightly appearance: both officers and men looked blue with the cold; and our long beards, with our wet and dirty clothing drying upon us, was anything but comfortable. As the morning advanced and all were in motion, one might imagine the plain itself to be undergoing a movement. Imagine seventy thousand men huddled together. The buzzing resembled the distant roar of the sea against a rocky coast."

Wellington's officers and men sought food and warmth with varying success. Some regiments were supplied with meat from the commissariat waggons, but most went without. Spirits had higher priority, and these seem to have reached the great majority of the army. Sergeant Wheeler's company was moved out of the mud at daylight and posted near some houses; "these we soon ghutted and what by the help of doors, windows, shutters and furniture, we soon made some good fires." They were not allowed to enjoy them for long, for by eight his brigade had gone into position.

The Rifle Brigade were old campaigners: "We made a fire against the wall of Sir Andrew Barnard's cottage", records Captain Kincaid, "and boiled a huge camp-kettle full of tea, mixed up with a suitable quantity of milk and sugar for breakfast, and, as it stood on the high-road, where all the big-wigs of the army had occasion to pass, in the early part of the morning, I believe almost every one of them, from the Duke downwards, claimed a cupful." Young Ensign Leeke's breakfast

> "consisted of a biscuit each and some soup, which was in one of the servants' mess tins; I was unintentionally on his part, done out of my drink of broth by one of the officers exclaiming, just as I put my lips to the tin, 'Come Master Leeke, I think you have had your share of that.' This half-mouthful of broth and a biscuit were all I tasted that day until after nine o'clock when I got a lump of bread as big as my fist from a French loaf."

The English troops began to take up their positions a little after six o'clock, but the numbers of men and horses engaged in the operation were so large that several hours passed before it was completed. As his brigades moved into line Wellington rode along the front carefully examining the ground, and supervising his commanders' arrangements. He had mounted his favourite horse, Copenhagen, which he had ridden at Vittoria and Toulouse, and he was dressed in the habitual dark blue coat, cloak, white breeches and white cravat. His cocked hat was without plumes, but bore four cockades, a large black one, King George's, and three smaller emblems in the colours of Portugal, Spain, and the Netherlands, the four armies in which he held the rank of Field-Marshal.

A mile away, across the valley, the Emperor's preparations were not nearly so far advanced, for he had not finished paying for his indecision on the previous morning. The bulk of the army had been a long way behind him when Napoleon began his headlong pursuit of the English on the afternoon of the 17th, and at nightfall they bivouacked several miles in the rear of the advance guard. Although Soult had sent out orders at 5 a.m. instructing the divisional commanders to have their troops ready and in position by nine o'clock, it was much later that the last of the French regiments arrived on the field. The Emperor breakfasted a little before eight in his headquarters at Le Caillou, with Soult, his Chief of Staff, Bassano, Drouot, and a number of other generals. His spirits were high, but his companions felt less optimistic of the chances of victory. Soult repeated his plea that some of Grouchy's troops should be recalled if they were to be sure of success. The Emperor assured him that he overrated Wellington's generalship and the value of the English army. Soult had fought the English in the Peninsula, and retained a healthy respect for the Duke and his men. "Because you have been beaten by Wellington", the Emperor retorted, "you consider him a great general. And now I tell you that Wellington is a bad general, that the English are bad troops, and that this affair is nothing more serious than eating one's breakfast." Napoleon's young brother Jérôme came into the room, accompanied by Reille, his corps commander.

Reille was asked his opinion as an old Peninsula campaigner, and to the Emperor's annoyance was even more pessimistic than Soult. "Well posted", said Reille, "as Wellington knows how to post it, and attacked from the front, the English infantry are unshakeable. . . . Before attacking it with the bayonet you may expect to have the attackers brought to the ground. But the English army is less agile, less supple, less expert in manœuvring than ours, and if we cannot beat it by a direct attack, we can do so by manœuvring." Napoleon was irritated by this depressing conclusion, and brought the conversation to an abrupt close, possibly because he did not wish the bystanders to become defeatist, possibly because he thought that Reille exaggerated the difficulties of fighting the English. Whatever his reasons, he ignored the advice, although he had never met the English army in action before, and he made no attempt that day to turn Wellington's front. Jérôme ventured to tell his brother that when dining at Genappe the night before, the hotel waiter had repeated to him a conversation overheard when one of Wellington's aides-de-camp had been having lunch there. The aide had said that Wellington and Blücher had agreed to join forces in front of the Forest of Soignes (that is, at Mont-Saint-Jean), and that the Prussian army would be marching via Wavre. This the Emperor flatly refused to believe, although it was the third time that the Prussians had been reported to be marching towards Wavre, and therefore within reach of the forthcoming battle, and he dismissed Jérôme's warning, firmly believing that after the battle of Ligny the Prussian army was in no shape to join the English as a fighting force for another two days.

Napoleon left the house, mounted his white arab Marengo, and rode down the road to examine the English position from La Belle Alliance. Although by now the rain had stopped and the sun was shining, the ground was still too sodden to allow easy manœuvring. He went back to the farm at Rossomme, where, at 10 a.m. seated at a table in the open air, he composed a despatch to Grouchy. "You will direct your movements upon Wavre, so as to approach us, act in concert with us, driving before you the Prussian army which has taken that route, and which may have halted at Wavre, where you must arrive as soon as possible." These orders establish the Emperor's share of the responsibility for Grouchy's failure to keep the Prussians away from the battle with the English.

In the first place, by the time Grouchy received his instructions— they reached him at 4 p.m.—the damage would be done: the Prussians would have joined Wellington. Secondly, if Napoleon imagined that Blücher was going to appear on his flank, the obvious step to take at 10 a.m. was to tell Grouchy to rejoin the army at once. The reason for the Emperor's delay in writing to Grouchy, and his failure to recall him when he did, was simply that he believed the Prussians were in no state to fight that afternoon. By one o'clock when Napoleon could see Blücher's advance guard for himself, he summoned Grouchy to join him immediately; this message reached the Marshal at 5 p.m. and his troops were already engaged with Blücher's rearguard; even if they had been free to march, they would not have arrived at Mont-Saint-Jean before nightfall.

Napoleon was directly responsible for most of the mistakes

Grouchy made of his own initiative. The Emperor's first instructions on the previous day had been vague and misleading; they were based on insufficient information because he had neglected to pursue the Prussians vigorously as they retreated from Ligny. In place of accurate intelligence Napoleon substituted wishful thinking; he was "making pictures" in the very manner which he delighted to criticise in his generals, and Grouchy was ordered to follow the Prussians "in the direction of Namur and Maestricht". The Marshal's critics have argued that when at Walhain, 16 miles off, he heard the first salvoes of the battle of Waterloo, he should have marched to the field without a moment's hesitation. Indeed, his subordinates urged him to do this, but Grouchy ignored their advice on the grounds that his orders were explicit and that he had to carry them out. The Emperor expected strict obedience to his instructions from semi-independent commanders like Grouchy, who were charged with the execution of an operation whose part in the grand strategical plan only the commander in chief could see wholly and clearly. It was Napoleon's fault that the orders were inadequate. Grouchy has been blamed, and with more justice, for his caution on the 18th, yet even here the Emperor must take some of the responsibility. He was in the rear of an enemy numbering 75,000 or twice his strength, and certainly not in the demoralised state Napoleon pictured to himself. Despite his difficulties, Grouchy did reach Wavre, and he might well have congratulated himself when the Emperor's morning despatch arrived at 4 p.m. for he had taken the town and defeated a Prussian corps to do so. In the meantime, however, Blücher's three other corps had gone to Wellington's assistance.

Having written to Grouchy, Napoleon left the farm at Rossomme to review his troops as they deployed for battle. This they did with characteristic *apparat*, with drums beating and the bands playing *Veillons au salut de l'Empire*. Six hundred yards away, within easy cannon range, Wellington's men watched the glittering display and listened to the music and the redoubled shouts of *Vive l'Empereur!* with more curiosity than emotion. At eleven, Napoleon dictated the brief instructions for his straightforward plan of battle. He chose a frontal assault because he was impatient to eliminate the English as quickly as possible, and a frontal attack

would be the speediest way of doing this. A flank movement
would be cheaper in lives, and possibly far more profitable, but to
be rejected on the score that it might well be indecisive. At one
o'clock, or very soon afterwards, by which time the whole of the
army should have arrived and be ready to take part, Ney was to
direct d'Erlon's corps to attack the road junction at Mont-Saint-
Jean, where the main Charleroi-Brussels road is crossed by the road
which runs along the ridge from Wavre to Braine-la-Leud. Intense
preliminary artillery bombardment would precede Ney's attack on
Mont-Saint-Jean, and when d'Erlon's corps went forward, Reille's
corps on the left would assault Wellington's right. These tactics
were barbarously unsubtle, for they envisaged smashing the centre
of the English front, doubtless at heavy cost, after which the rest
of the army would rapidly exploit the breach in the enemy's line.

When Napoleon began his career as a general in Italy he was
already a past master in the art of taking calculated risks in battle;
by the time he ended it in Belgium nineteen years later his tactics
were more those of a gambler than a soldier. He retained his skill
as a strategist to the end—the opening of his last campaign was
brilliant—but on the battlefield he now exchanged stratagem for
brute force. In his choice of frontal assault on Wellington's lines
are all the gambler's compulsive refusal to face realities and capacity
for self-delusion. On the morning of the 18th of June he wrote
off the Prussians on the slenderest of evidence, he disparaged the
English army and its commander although his generals had warned
him to respect them, and he ignored the strength of the position
Wellington had chosen to defend. At breakfast time he told his
officers that he thought that his chances of victory were ninety out
of a hundred, although he believed, erroneously, that the English
outnumbered him. Frontal attacks had won quick victories before,
at a heavy price, but these had been against unreliable troops, and
although some of Wellington's regiments were poor material the
best of them could be expected to hold their ground stubbornly.
Yet the Emperor refused to manœuvre as Reille urged him to do in
the light of French experience in the Peninsula; doubtless he
rejected the idea because it seemed less likely to bring him the
decisive victory he so desperately needed. The facts of the situation
scarcely justify his decision; the English stood a strong chance of

holding him at bay for many hours, possibly till nightfall. If he failed to carry their lines his reverse would be so great that there might not be a second opportunity to win the campaign, while if he decided to manœuvre and failed to turn Wellington's front, his army would be left virtually intact, and his position would still not be beyond redemption. Had Napoleon been able to make a dispassionate appreciation of his situation before Mont-Saint-Jean he would have realised that if he succeeded in battering his way through the English centre it would be by such a small margin that he would have risked all to gain all; there was at least as much chance of winning the battle by manœuvre, and far less risk attached to it. He denied himself his army's greatest strength, its mobility, he gave away the enemy's weakest point, its lack of flexibility, when he chose a frontal assault. He could not have placed more faith in his star and his troops' willingness to sacrifice their lives.

Wellington's preparations for the battle might seem to belong to a different world; they were as foreign to his opponent as the methods and habits and outlook of his army were removed from Napoleon's. The Emperor had walked for so long amongst vast enterprises of state as well as war that he had ceased to concern himself with the details Wellington bore constantly in mind. No man has ever shown more capacity for labour or rapidity of decision, but in doubling the rôles of Commander-in-Chief and Head of State he was obliged to give his officers far more independence than the Duke ever dreamt of allowing his. When he led the largest army the world had seen, at the height of his power, the task of directing that alone was too great for personal control. He became increasingly a modern Supreme Commander, issuing broad directives to his Marshals, and intervening only in cases of special difficulty. The Emperor's heaviest burdens were no longer in the field; he supervised the operations in distant theatres of war, he continued to rule France and her satellites as an autocrat through whose hands the issues of government must pass uninterruptedly for settlement. The Marshals were left more and more to their own devices, and lacking their master's genius, they made mistakes which had to be redeemed at the cost of fresh losses.

Unable to devote himself as he once had to the battles on which his power depended, Napoleon came to count on mere numbers to compensate for his preoccupation and his subordinates' shortcomings. The war with Europe was reduced to a killing match where muster rolls mattered more than skill; fresh levies were raised to supplement the veterans of the revolutionary armies and replace the mounting losses of the new sledge-hammer tactics. After 1812 France paid the price of her numerical inferiority in a series of catastrophic defeats, in which Napoleon continued to meet force with force until his armies melted almost entirely away. He was left at last with what he began his career—a handful of troops and his incomparable gift for war. With them he performed prodigies in the last weeks of his first reign, but his numbers were too small to affect the issue, despite his successes. The apostle of mass had become its victim.

At Waterloo Napoleon's army was more manageable than it had been at the height of the Empire, but the practices of the old days still held good. The Commander-in-Chief maintained his political correspondence, determined the strategy, brought his troops skilfully to the battlefield, where he dictated a general plan which repeated the bloody formulae of the later years, and left his subordinates to see to the rest. Wellington had always been short of troops, had forgone any victories which might have reduced his strength to danger point, and was accustomed to concentrate the control of a battle in his own hands.

Economy had been enforced on the Duke during the long years in the Peninsula and it befitted his temperament, which was practical and empiric to a degree. He had an unrivalled grasp of fighting tactics, and long experience in combining them in defence. He had never been able to risk initial ambitious offensives, for he had usually been outnumbered, and obliged to win a defensive victory before he could campaign on an equal footing with his enemy. Wellington exploited his men's traditions and training to the full, for they were of the same defensive-offensive nature as his own tactics. His long acquaintance with his army had not inspired great love, on either side, but it had created a common confidence, and a ready understanding of his purposes. Such was his commanders' familiarity with his methods and the kind of terrain they had to defend at Waterloo, that it was sufficient for the Duke to order them to dispose their troops as usual. They made the best of any cover in the firing line itself, and stationed their reserves on the reverse slope to protect them from the French artillery. Strong points in front of the line along the ridge were to be held and fortified as much as time and materials allowed. The final decision on any arrangement lay in Wellington's hands, and as he moved along the front on his tour of inspection he made a number of valuable modifications. Lord Uxbridge, the second-in-command, rode up to ask what the Duke's plans were in case he should be left to execute them. "Plans!" replied Wellington, "I have no plans. I shall be guided by circumstances."

The Duke's tactics at Waterloo were sounder than his strategy that day, for he decided to leave 17,000 men and thirty guns eight miles from the battlefield at Hal and Tubize. Wellington had begun the campaign so convinced that Napoleon would march via Mons on Brussels and his lines of communication with the sea, that his first orders for the concentration of the army were designed to meet this threat. On grounds of principle alone, there was little reason to warrant the Emperor with such a plan of campaign, and the early reports of his progress made it clear that he was heading for the allies' weakest point, the junction of their armies around Charleroi. By midnight on the 15th the Duke himself could see that he had been mistaken, and altered his concentration area to Quatre Bras. Nevertheless, more than two days later, at Waterloo, he remained so apprehensive of an indirect attack on his rear that he detached a fifth of his army to forestall such a development. At the same time he felt his numbers to be too small to fight at Mont-Saint-Jean without the assistance of one of Blücher's corps. Not unnaturally, in later years Wellington always defended his provisions at Hal and Tubize as wise; they would have made more sense if he had been much nearer the coast. As it was, the French could hardly have marched on the distant ports before the Duke could place himself in their path, and with this in mind, the importance of Hal and Tubize becomes very small indeed; "it is difficult to comprehend", wrote Kennedy, eyewitness and historian of the campaign, "how any French force could have got to Tubize and Hal without its advance being previously known." Wellington's preoccupation with his far right seems very strange in the light of the urgent situation on his immediate front, where the French army were massed to attack. It cannot even be said that the Duke was paying attention to the danger of the French employing their skill at manœuvre, because his detachment was too far off to join the battle, and if the Emperor were to turn the enemy's flank during the engagement, it would be his left, which was much the weaker: the Prussians were still far off on the morning of the 18th. There were so many better uses to which those 17,000 troops might have been put. They could have been brought in to manœuvre against the Emperor's left flank, and thus draw off some of the forces which would otherwise be sent against the English at Mont-Saint-Jean. Alternatively, they might have reinforced the main army so that it was strong enough to hold off the Emperor indefinitely, until Blücher arrived to give the allies a crushing numerical superiority, and victory. This aspect of the battle has received small popular attention because Wellington was victorious, but the Duke had no more reason for leaving so many men and guns at Hal and Tubize than Napoleon had for failing to recall Grouchy during the night of the 17th.

The Waterloo position was admirably suited to Wellington's methods; it was also one of the smallest battlefields of the era, a consideration which goes some way to explain the severity of the casualties suffered by both sides. A glance at the map (p. 124) is sufficient to make its geography and the placing of the two armies quite clear. The area is bisected from north to south by the main road from Brussels to Charleroi, Napoleon's line of operations. The road runs from Brussels through the Forest of Soignes, past the village of Waterloo and enters open country before climbing the gentle reverse slope up to the ridge overlooking the battlefield. Just beyond the crest it passes the farm of La Haye Sainte, after which it descends into the valley separating the two armies, and continues its route to Charleroi via Genappe, Quatre Bras and Gosselies. The hamlet of Mont-Saint-Jean stands at the foot of the reverse slope, three-quarters of a mile to the north of the ridge, at the junction of the road from Nivelles with the chaussée from Brussels to Charleroi. From Mont-Saint-Jean the route to Nivelles passes behind the Château of Hougoumont, which Wellington had fortified in front of his right wing, and a quarter of a mile to the south of Hougoumont it marks the limit of Napoleon's left flank. A much simpler, unpaved road played a greater part in the battle than the two which meet at Mont-Saint-Jean. It lies a thousand yards south of the hamlet, and runs from Wavre to Braine-la-Leud along the crest which Wellington had chosen for his first line of defence. Three hundred yards to the north of La Belle Alliance it crosses the chaussée from Brussels. To the east of the junction in Wellington's centre, in the direction of Wavre, the side road was bordered by thick high hedges, offering excellent cover, while to the west, towards Braine-la-Leud, it ran through a cutting 5 to 6 feet deep, of the sort commonly found in this part of Belgium, and even more suitable for defence than the hedges in the other half of the line. Wellington's officers pierced these hedges and cuttings at intervals along the front to allow the passage of the cavalry and artillery.

The valley between the two armies is never more than twelve hundred yards in breadth, and is shallow and undulating. The extreme length of the battlefield, from Paris Wood to Braine-la-Leud is only four miles, and its effective length much shorter still. It was a small area in which to employ 400 guns and 140,000 men. The terrain was best described by Houssaye: "Seen from La Belle Alliance the main road to Brussels, which goes up and down again in a straight line, seems very steep. But this is an illusion of perspective. In reality the inclination of the slope is not very great. A horseman can ascend it at an even gallop without straining his horse or putting it out of breath. However, to the right as well as to the left of the road, the ground is extremely uneven, and in many places becomes steep. It is an infinite succession of mounds and hollows, of depressions and banks, of furrows and hillocks. Nevertheless, when viewed from a height, the double valley has the aspect of a plain extending without any marked depressions between two low hills. It is necessary to walk over the ground to perceive the constantly undulating formation of the ground, similar to the billows of a swelling sea."

The two outposts at Hougoumont and La Haye Sainte added enormously to the natural strength of Wellington's position, as the bitterness of the fighting around them, and the consequences of the eventual fall of La Haye Sainte bear out. On the left of the

20   *The Battle (note the rockets; see p. 34)*

From an aquatint by R. Reeve after a drawing by W. Heath, 1816

21 "The Exterior of Hougoumont at the commencement of the Battle of Waterloo"
(The building appears as it was after the Battle had been in progress for some hours)

From an engraving by T. Sutherland, 1816

main road from Brussels, after it has topped the ridge, but before it descends to the bottom of the valley, lay the sandpit Mercer passed before he halted on the eve of the battle. Opposite the sandpit stood the farmhouse and orchard of La Haye Sainte. 1,100 yards to the west and 500 yards in front of the English right wing stationed along the ridge road were the château, garden, orchard and wood of Hougoumont. Advanced posts of lesser importance than Hougoumont and La Haye Sainte were established at La Haye and Papelotte. Wellington's defences presented a formidable obstacle to the French army. The strong points would inflict casualties on the besiegers out of all proportion to the size of the garrisons, and as long as they remained unreduced would be a constant thorn in the side of every assault that by-passed them. The strength of their defences could only be overcome if the Emperor were willing to tie up large numbers of the troops who would otherwise have been used in the attack on the centre of the line. Behind the outposts were the extensive ready-made defences of hedges and banks of Wellington's front line. Behind these the sloping ground afforded shelter from gunfire for the Duke's second line of reserves. Here lay sufficient roads and the best drained ground of the field on which to move his forces rapidly to threatened stretches of the front.

So strong was Wellington's position that it might seem that his task in defending it with 67,661 men and 156 guns against the Emperor's 71,947 and 246 guns was an easy one, but the near equality in numbers was illusory. At the end of the battle, fought on his terms, the Duke declared that it was the closest run thing he had ever seen. Napoleon's troops were veterans and their enthusiasm at its height; Wellington's a strange and fearful collection of Germans, Belgians, Dutch and English, of whom he could only safely trust the first and the last. The more reliable regiments were largely a scratch collection of second battalions, stiffened by only a scattering of Peninsular veterans who had not been sent to North America in 1814. Before the day ended thousands of his allied troops, many of whom had served under the Emperor not long before, had left the battle. The majority of those who stayed were under fire for the first time. For this very reason they laid down their lives when the older hands thought it more prudent to

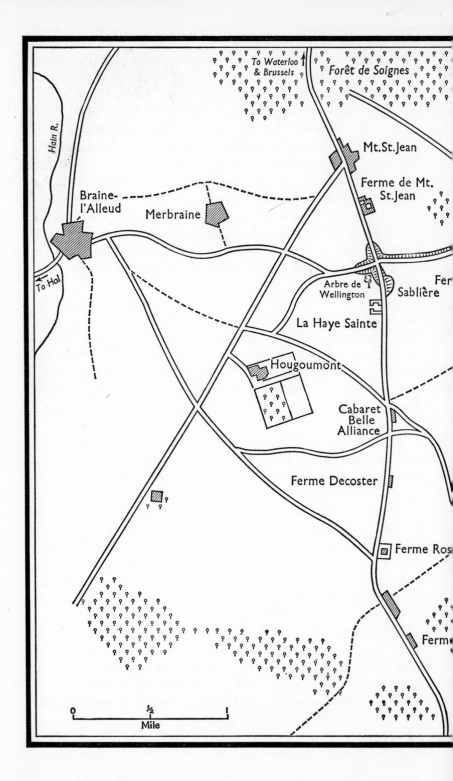

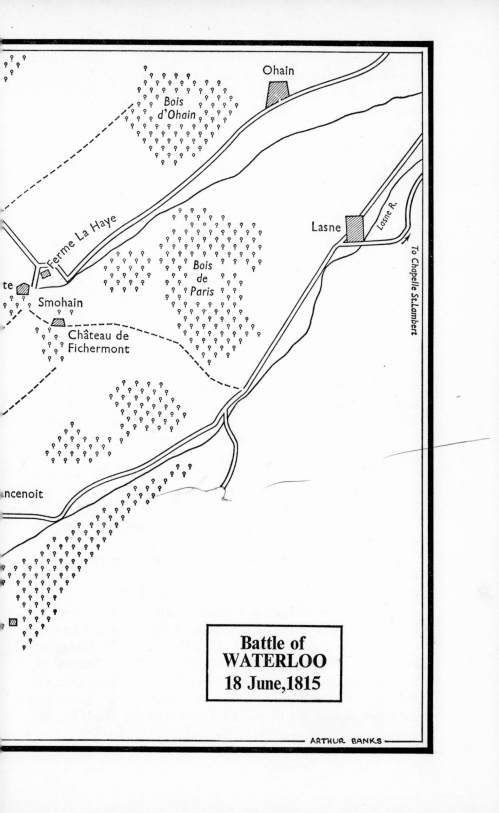

Ohain

Bois
d'Ohain

Ferme La Haye

Lasne

Lasne R.

To Chapelle St.Lambert

Bois
de
Paris

te

Smohain

Château de
Fichermont

ncenoit

Battle of
WATERLOO
18 June,1815

ARTHUR BANKS

remain where they were or to retire. The courage and desperation of the recruits were no substitute for the seasoned campaigners Wellington had commanded in Spain. If he had only had his old army, concluded the Duke, criticising Napoleon's bull-headed tactics at Waterloo, he would have swept his opponents off the face of the earth in a couple of hours. "This", said Kincaid of the Rifle Brigade,

> "was the last, the greatest, and the most uncomfortable heap of glory that I ever had a hand in, and may the deuce take me if I think that everybody waited there to see the end of it, otherwise it never could have been so troublesome to those who did. We were, take us all in all, a very bad army. Our foreign auxiliaries, who constituted more than half our numerical strength, with some exceptions, were little better than a raw militia—a body without a soul, or like an inflated pillow, that gives to the touch and resumes its shape again when the pressure ceases—not to mention the many who went clear out of the field, and were only seen while plundering our baggage in their retreat."

The state of the ground and the late arrival of the last of his troops had obliged the Emperor to abandon his hopes of an early start to the battle. A little after eleven he ordered the great battery of 80 guns then massing to the right of La Belle Alliance to deliver the preliminary cannonade at noon. At one o'clock d'Erlon's infantry were to move forward in a grand assault on Wellington's centre. Napoleon decided to assist d'Erlon's troops by staging a diversion beforehand against Hougoumont. This was to be a demonstration rather than a costly attack, but he hoped that it would alarm the Duke sufficiently to withdraw men from his centre in order to strengthen his right.

Reille, whose corps faced Hougoumont, was instructed to send one of his divisions to assault the château, and at 11.35 Jérôme's divisional batteries fired the first shots of the battle of Waterloo. After the customary barrage, a cloud of skirmishers, followed by four regiments of infantry marched down the slopes and into the outskirts of Hougoumont wood. The defenders fought stubbornly, it took an hour to clear the wood, and as the French emerged on the other side, they were greeted by volleys of musketry from the thick walls of the château. Reille sent instructions to Jérôme that the attack should not be pushed farther than the wood, but the

Emperor's young brother called up fresh battalions in an attempt
to capture the buildings. No movements were observed from the
English centre; Napoleon's feint attack had drawn in the French,
not the enemy. Not content with persisting in a bloody assault
whose sole purpose had been to mislead the enemy, Jérôme pressed
it home recklessly. Instead of reducing the buildings' thick walls
by howitzer fire, he threw in more and more infantry. Their courage
deserved better tactics, for repeated attempts to storm the walls
left only fresh heaps of dead, shot down as they approached, or
bayoneted as they attempted to clamber over the six feet of masonry
surrounding the château. Throughout the French lines that day
the troops executed equally sterile tactics with the same heroism,
at the orders of older and more experienced commanders than
Jérôme.

For the first hour and a half the battle was confined to the
struggle at Hougoumont and the artillery duel which traversed it.
At one o'clock the battery of 80 guns near La Belle Alliance had
still not begun the cannonade in preparation for d'Erlon's assault.
At last the Emperor received Ney's message announcing that the
preparations were complete, and before ordering the cannon-fire
which would fill the air with smoke, he turned his glass in a last
sweep of the horizon. He caught sight of what appeared to be a
black cloud emerging from the woods of Chapelle-Saint-Lambert,
6 miles away. The distance was too great to distinguish whose
troops they were, but he was not left long in doubt.

A captured Prussian cavalry subaltern was brought before
Napoleon. He was the bearer of a letter from Bülow to Wellington,
reporting the arrival of the Prussian 4th Corps at Chapelle-Saint-
Lambert. "Our whole army", the prisoner told Napoleon, "passed
last night at Wavre. We have seen no French, and suppose they
have marched on Plancenoit." This alarming news did not come as
a complete surprise to the Emperor; a despatch had been received
nearly two hours before from Grouchy which should have made
him realise at last how likely it was that the Prussians would intervene. It was timed Gembloux, 6 a.m.

"Sire,

All my reports and information confirm the fact that the
enemy is retiring upon Brussels, either to concentrate there,

or to give battle after uniting with Wellington. . . . They must have started from Tourinnes yesterday evening at half-past eight, and have marched all night; fortunately, the weather in the night was so wretched that they cannot have advanced very far. I am going to start immediately for Sart-à-Walhain whence I shall proceed to Corbais and Wavre."

This message ought to have convinced Napoleon beyond all reasonable doubt that Blücher was marching to join Wellington and that Grouchy had been terribly slow in following him. With such a start the Prussians must reach the battlefield unchecked. The situation had become so dangerous that the Marshal should have been sent an immediate summons to return, yet Napoleon was so unconcerned that he delayed answering Grouchy for almost two hours, until, in fact, a few minutes before Bülow's advance guard was identified on the heights of Chapelle-Saint-Lambert. When he did write, it was in such complaisant terms that clearly the Emperor could still not bring himself to believe that the Prussians were able to fight; not until Bülow's troops appeared did he finally wake from his self-delusion.

"Your movement", ran the message,

"from Corbais to Wavre agrees with His Majesty's arrangements. Nevertheless, the Emperor requests me to tell you that you must keep manœuvring in our direction, and seek to draw nearer to the army before any corps places itself between us. I do not indicate any special direction to you. It is for you to ascertain the point where we are, to act accordingly, to keep up our communications, and to see that you are in a position to fall upon and annihilate any of the enemy's troops which might try to molest our right."

The appearance of von Bülow added a clearer and more urgent postscript to Soult's vague instructions:

"A letter which has just been intercepted tells us that General Bülow is to attack our right flank. We believe that we can perceive this corps on the heights of Chapelle-Saint-Lambert. Therefore do not lose a minute to draw nearer to us and crush Bülow, whom you will catch in the very act."

The Emperor remained extraordinarily complacent in the flurry caused by the sight of the Prussian advance guard. He summoned Grouchy to rejoin the army at once, but this would take so long that at one o'clock it was almost a waste of time. The despatch arrived at Wavre at 5 p.m. where the Marshal had his hands full with Thielmann's Corps; if he had been free to march at once, he could not have reached Napoleon until well after nightfall. More alarming even than Grouchy's inability to return was the evidence of Blücher's concentration at Wavre. Having massed his army, the Prussian commander would be able to leave one corps to cover his rear while the rest of his forces made their way to Mont-Saint-Jean.

The Emperor refused to believe his battle with the English compromised, probably because he could not bring himself to jettison his plan of campaign and attempt the almost impossible task of separating and defeating the allies afresh. He may have decided that however desperate his situation might be, the alternatives were even worse. Whatever his reasons, he still declared himself confident of the outcome of the battle. The majority of Blücher's army must still be at Wavre, where Grouchy would pin it down miles from the decisive engagement with Wellington. Quite possibly the Marshal had already acted on his own initiative and was now marching on Bülow's rear at Plancenoit, as the captured Prussian subaltern thought. The English would be disposed of in good time to meet any serious threat from Blücher. "This morning", Napoleon assured Soult, "we had ninety chances in our favour. We still have sixty to forty, and if Grouchy repairs the terrible mistake he made in amusing himself at Gembloux, and marches rapidly, our victory will be all the more decisive, for Bülow's corps will be completely destroyed." In the meantime the Emperor took some precautions; he sent off two cavalry divisions to form a screen in Bülow's path, and behind them he deployed Lobau's 6th Corps to hold the Prussians back until Grouchy took them in the rear.

These arrangements took thirty minutes to complete, and it was not until half-past one that the battery opened fire. Wellington's artillery answered immediately. The cannonade lasted half an hour, but few of the shells reached the English troops because they were lying down in the shelter of the road embankments and the slope behind, and only one brigade, Bylandt's, suffered heavy casualties; for some unknown reason they had been left exposed to the French guns. At about two o'clock the battery stopped firing while d'Erlon's corps marched forward; as soon as the infantry had descended the valley, the guns resumed their salvoes.

Commanded by Ney and d'Erlon, four excellent divisions, Allix, Donzelot, Marcognet and Durutte's, in all 18,000 men, advanced over the uneven ground to Wellington's lines. Unfortunately for the Emperor, he had left the conduct of this grand assault in the hands of Ney and d'Erlon. An abundance of good cavalry was available for the attack, but it was scarcely used. Where the horsemen did appear their success underlined the mistake of not sending them up to the allied front in force. Had they arrived there just before the infantry approached, Wellington's men would have had to form squares to defend themselves; within minutes the defenders' fire power would have been reduced to a fraction. The French infantry went forward unprotected, and as they topped the ridge they were confronted by every musket in the lines which rose to meet them.

If Ney and d'Erlon had confined themselves to this single element-ary blunder all might yet have been well, but they chose to deploy three of the four divisions in a formation that had scarcely been seen for the last quarter of a century, and which was, moreover, more than normally inadvisable in the light of the ground the troops had to cover. The usual battalion column formation possessed a good many disadvantages when used against well-trained infantry, but it was a better one than the two commanders chose now; it could deploy into line fairly quickly, and if attacked by cavalry could soon form squares. Ney and d'Erlon formed up three-quarters of their infantry not in battalion columns, but divisional columns, each a battalion wide, so that the divisions were arranged in columns each the width of a battalion drawn up in three ranks. There were roughly 600 men in a battalion, and eight or nine battalions in a division. This made the columns 200 men wide and 24 to 27 ranks deep. It was impossible to deploy them quickly, and there could not have been a formation more vulnerable to case- and round-shot fire.

Wellington had taken up his position at the foot of a large elm tree*

---

* Some years after the battle the tree was purchased by an Englishman, who had it cut down and made into souvenirs.

22 "*The Interior of Hougoumont*"

From an engraving by T. Sutherland, 1817

23   *General Sir Colin Halkett*

Detail of the portrait by Jan Willem Pieneman

24   *Sir Thomas Picton*

Detail of the portrait by Sir William Beechey

which stood at the junction of the ridge road from Braine-la-
Leud to Wavre with the main road from Brussels to Charleroi
A few hundred yards before him down the main road to Charleroi.
lay La Haye Sainte and the sand pit. The gap between the farm and
sand pit had been closed by a barricade, and the post garrisoned
by Major Baring and a battalion of the German Legion. As d'Erlon's
infantry cleared the depression between the two armies the battery
near La Belle Alliance ceased fire; the enormous mass of 18,000
troops began to climb up to the plateau, forcing their way through
the uncut rye which covered the slopes. Their unwieldy divisional
columns made excellent targets for the Duke's artillery, but they
continued to advance steadily, undeterred by the numerous gaps
which appeared in their ranks. "No man was ever better served
by his soldiers", said Napoleon at St. Helena, of the battle of
Waterloo, and despite their crippling formations, d'Erlon's men
attacked with such resolution that they brought Wellington closer
to defeat than did any of the other assaults that day.

The four divisions attacked at intervals along the front, Donzelot
accompanied by a brigade of cavalry at La Haye Sainte, then Allix
and Marcognet in the centre, and finally Durutte on the far left at
Papelotte. Ney and d'Erlon marched at the head of Allix's column.
The English skirmishers fell back to the front line; Allix and
Marcognet's divisions pressed on through a storm of gunfire
until they came up to Bylandt's Dutch Belgian Brigade, the only
body Wellington had left on the forward slope exposed to the enemy
artillery, and swept it before them. Bylandt's routed troops streamed
back through the lines of the Cameron Highlanders lying down
behind the crest awaiting the command to appear in front of the
unsuspecting French. On the left Durutte's division took Papelotte
without great difficulty. The Germans in La Haye Sainte fought
off an attempt to storm the buildings, and the majority of Donzelot's
division passed on to deliver the assault on the lines behind it.
Ignoring the protests of his staff, Wellington remained under the
elm tree until the sand pit had fallen and the French skirmishers
started to fire from the garden of La Haye Sainte. In the centre
the French had now reached the top of the ridge, and from where
the Emperor stood at Rossomme it seemed as if the English line
was about to collapse.

Donzelot's leading troops were allowed to advance almost to the hedges bordering the road before Picton ordered his division to rise and move forward. The column halted just below the crest of the slope to deploy, and as Donzelot and his officers were struggling to complete this difficult task, a cheer was heard along the ridge above them. Less than 40 yards away stood the English infantry, their line extending far on either side of Donzelot's confused column. The English raised their muskets, a massed volley struck the attackers who wavered under a heavy fire which few of them were able to return. Picton ordered the charge, and fell almost at once with a bullet through his temple; his men poured down the slope driving Donzelot's troops before them.

Elsewhere the abrupt appearance of infantry and a hail of musket fire had brought the French advance to a standstill. Detachments of cavalry were at last approaching to support d'Erlon's regiments; within minutes they would force the English to go into square and the advantage would return to the French. The Highlanders had already begun to form squares when Uxbridge threw his cavalry into the struggle, overwhelming the infantry and the numerically inferior cuirassiers supporting them. Surrounded by Vandeleur's dragoons, Durutte's division withdrew from Papelotte in reasonable order. Elsewhere the French were unable to stem the tide of horsemen which poured down from the ridge.

On the central slopes the cuirassiers were swept from d'Erlon's flanks, leaving the dense crowds of infantry almost defenceless, for their formations did not allow more than a small number to fire on the cavalry who rode into them sabring at will. Many who managed to extricate themselves from the columns were ridden down as they fled. D'Erlon's force broke into numerous groups which retreated towards their lines beset by the exultant cavalry and a number of infantry which had followed them in the counter-attack.

Sergeant Ewart of the Greys captured the eagle and standard of the 45th Regiment of the Line:

> "It was in the charge I took the eagle from the enemy: he and I had a hard contest for it; he made a thrust at my groin, I parried it off and cut him down through the head. After this a lancer came at me; I threw the lance off by my right side, and cut him through the chin and upwards through the teeth. Next, a foot-soldier fired at me, and then charged me with

his bayonet, which I also had the good luck to parry, and then I cut him down through the head; thus ended the contest. As I was about to follow my regiment, the general said, 'My brave fellow, take that to the rear; you have done enough till you get quit of it.' I took the eagle to the ridge and afterwards to Brussels."*

Flushed with their success, Somerset and Ponsonby's cavalry threw all restraint to the winds, and ignoring Uxbridge's call to return, charged on across the valley and up the opposite slope. For a few minutes, until they were overwhelmed by the Emperor's fresh cavalry and infantry, they rode along his front, sabring everyone they could reach, and silencing thirty guns of the great battery by cutting down the gun crews. Ponsonby's horse sank in ploughland, and he and his aide-de-camp were killed by a handful of lancers before they could be rescued.

One in three of the cavalry who took part in the counter-attack remained on the ground when it was over; Wellington had lost 2,500 of his horsemen, a quarter of his entire cavalry. Most of these losses had been to no purpose, they were largely sustained by the troops who had joined the headlong rush on the Emperor's line when the real business of the charge was over; Ponsonby's brigade had been almost destroyed for its foolhardiness. The Duke had begun the battle with dangerously inferior numbers of cavalry, and unless he were extremely lucky he would have to pay dearly for their disobedience as the afternoon wore on.

Nevertheless, the first great crisis of the battle had been surmounted; 3,000 prisoners had been taken, not to mention the casualties d'Erlon's corps had suffered in their unsuccessful assault, and for the moment the slopes in front of the English lines had been swept clear of the enemy. As Lord Uxbridge returned to the ridge regretting his needless losses, he met "the Duke of Wellington, surrounded by all the *corps diplomatique militaire*, who from the high ground had witnessed the whole affair. The plain appeared to be swept clean, and I never saw so joyous a group as this *troupe dorée*. They thought the battle was over."

It was now three o'clock, and for a while the battle died down,

---

* Ewart was an outstanding swordsman, as his account suggests. He was 6 foot 4 inches and exceptionally strong. He was commissioned in the following year and died in 1845, aged seventy-seven.

except at Hougoumont, where the struggle continued with mounting violence. Attack was met by counter-attack. Wellington sent three companies of infantry to reinforce the defenders, and Napoleon ordered Jérôme to use howitzers to breach the walls. Part of the buildings caught fire, trapping the wounded in the flames.

7

Waterloo: Afternoon

WELLINGTON HAD LOST a quarter of his cavalry in the first
ninety minutes' fighting, and Bylandt's 3,000 men were now unfit
for further action, but the advantage rested with him and not the
Emperor. D'Erlon's defeat had strengthened the delicate morale of
some of the allied troops, and thousands of French had been
sacrificed without gaining a single foothold for the next assault.
At Hougoumont 1,200 men continued to hold off many times
their number; La Haye Sainte remained unreduced several hundreds
of yards in front of the English centre, and the whole length of
the slopes would have to be mounted once more in the teeth of the
allied batteries. Wellington's greatest gain had been in time; he
had only to preserve his position until the Prussians arrived, and
when the enemy attacked him again they would be two hours
closer.

Grouchy's latest despatch had just reached Napoleon; it was
timed Walhain, 11.30. Walhain is 9 miles from Wavre; evidently
Grouchy had still not grasped the urgency of the situation; the
Prussians were free to manœuvre as they pleased, and there could
now be no hope of the Marshal appearing on the battlefield before
nightfall. The Emperor was in the position of a poker player holding
a reasonable hand who suddenly realises from the speed with which
the other players raise the stakes instead of falling out of the round,
that his cards stand little chance of winning when at last they are
put on the table. But he could not cut his losses by throwing in
his hand; he had already staked more than he could afford to lose,
and he was forced to remain in the game, uneasily covering each
rise in the stakes, increasingly aware that the cost, if he lost, would
be catastrophic. To retreat from the battle at 3.30 would have

been to abandon the campaign, and to do this would be political suicide. If he wished to continue the battle it would be against greater odds with every hour that passed; together the English and Prussians outnumbered him two to one. Wellington must be defeated before the Prussians arrived in force, and with the troops which remained when detachments had been posted to hold back Blücher's vanguard. Ney was therefore to seize La Haye Sainte as quickly as possible, and from this advanced post a second grand assault would be made by d'Erlon's and Reille's corps together with the cavalry and the fresh infantry of the Guard.

This operation got off to a poor start, and as if to flout the Emperor's intentions altogether, Ney soon lost sight of his vital objective in a fit of recklessness which committed the bulk of the French cavalry without support long before it should have been used. He resumed the attack on La Haye Sainte with only two battalions of infantry. D'Erlon's corps had been seriously disorganised by their repulse from the ridge and the cavalry pursuit which followed. At Hougoumont Reille's corps had become thoroughly embroiled in a struggle which had now been going on for four hours, and Reille found it difficult to extricate troops to send to Ney. The two battalions proved quite inadequate for the task of clearing the outpost, and were driven off without much trouble. This reverse did not disconcert Ney as much as it might have done, for he had glimpsed through the clouds of dense smoke which overhung Wellington's centre all the signs of a considerable movement to the rear; evidently the allied line was crumbling, a prompt attack should be sufficient to carry it. What he actually saw were wounded soldiers and empty ammunition waggons leaving the firing line; Wellington was strengthening this section of his front, not weakening it. Ney sent for cavalry to seize this opportunity of finishing the battle, and deciding that the urgency of the situation did not give him time to obtain the Emperor's approval, ordered up Milhaud's two divisions of cuirassiers. Launching such numbers of cavalry against unbroken infantry was a serious blunder; it became a disaster when Lefebvre-Desnouettes, whose division was in the rear of Milhaud's divisions decided to join them without consulting any of his superiors.

Wellington's men formed squares to receive this fresh assault, scarcely believing it possible that the enemy would be so rash as to send thousands of cavalry against them without first mounting an infantry attack and providing adequate artillery support. The gunners were instructed to abandon their guns when the cuirassiers were upon them and take shelter in the squares. In later years the Duke was fond of criticising the commanders who disobeyed his repeated instructions on this point by withdrawing their batteries when the cavalry came near and who were consequently unable to return to the line in time to fire at the retreating horsemen. Such exceptions were few; by and large Wellington's gunners gave him outstanding service at Waterloo; he would not have found a better artillery corps in Europe. Nevertheless, his coolness to the artillery was notorious, and he allowed it to blind him to their share in his victory. Mercer neither entered the squares nor retired his guns when the French arrived at the crest, and so achieved the distinction of being probably the only battery commander who was able to drive them off unaided. As we shall see, he had good reasons for his disobedience:

"It might have been, as nearly as I can recollect, about 3 p.m. when Sir Augustus Frazer galloped up, crying out, 'Left limber up, and as fast as you can.' The words were scarcely uttered when my gallant troop stood as desired in column of subdivisions, left in front, pointing towards the main ridge. 'At a gallop, march!' and away we flew, as steadily and as compactly as if at a review. I rode with Frazer, whose face was as black as a chimney sweep's from the smoke, and the jacket-sleeve of his right arm torn open by a musket-ball or case shot, which had merely grazed his flesh. As we went along, he told me that the enemy had assembled an enormous mass of heavy cavalry in front of the point to which he was leading us (about one third of the distance between Hougou-mont and the Charleroi road), and that in all probability we should be immediately charged on gaining our position. '*The Duke's orders, however, are positive*', he added, '*that in the event of their persevering and charging home, you do not expose your men, but retire with them into the adjacent squares of infantry.*' As he spoke, we were ascending the reverse slope of the main position. We breathed a new atmosphere—the air was suffocatingly hot, resembling that issuing from an oven. We were enveloped in thick smoke, and *malgré* the incessant roar of cannon and musketry, could distinctly hear around us a mysterious humming noise, like that which one hears of a summer's evening proceeding from myriads of black beetles; cannon-shot, too, ploughed the ground in all directions, and so thick was the hail of balls and bullets that it seemed dangerous to extend the arm lest it should be torn off. In spite of the serious situation in which we were, I could not help being somewhat amused at the astonishment expressed by our kind-hearted surgeon (Hitchens), who heard for the first time this kind of music. He was close to me as we ascended the slope and, hearing this infernal carillon about his ears, began staring around in the wildest and most comic manner imaginable, twisting himself from side to side, exclaiming 'My God, Mercer, what *is* that? What *is* all this noise? How curious!—how very curious!' And then when a cannon-shot rushed hissing past, 'There!—there! What *is* it all?' It was with great difficulty that I persuaded him to retire: for a time he insisted in remaining near me, and it was only by pointing out how important it was to us, in case of being wounded, that he should keep himself safe to be able to assist us, that I prevailed upon him to withdraw. Amidst this storm we gained the summit of the ridge, strange to say, without a casualty; and Sir Augustus, pointing out our position between two squares of Brunswick infantry, left us with injunctions to remember the Duke's order, and to economise our ammunition. The Brunswickers were falling fast—the shot every moment making great gaps in their squares, which the officers and sergeants were actively employed in filling up by pushing their men together, and sometimes thumping them ere they would move. These were the very boys whom I had but yesterday seen throwing away their arms, and fleeing, panicstricken, from the very sound of our horses' feet. Today they fled not bodily, to be sure, but spiritually, for their senses seemed to have left them. There they stood, with recovered arms, like so many logs, or rather like the very wooden figures which I had seen them practising at in their cantonments. Every moment I feared that they would again throw down their arms and flee; but their officers and sergeants behaved nobly, not only keeping them together, but managing to keep their squares closed in spite of the carnage made amongst them. To have sought refuge amongst men in such a state were madness—the very moment our men ran from their guns, I was convinced, would be the signal for their disbanding. We had better, then, fall at our posts than in such a situation. Our coming up seemed to reanimate them, and all their eyes were directed to us—indeed, it was providential, for, had we not arrived as we did, I scarcely think there is a doubt of what would have been their fate.*

"Our first gun had scarcely gained the interval between their

* (Mercer's footnote.) "That the Duke was not ignorant of their danger I have from Captain Baynes, our Brigade Major, who told me that after Sir Augustus Frazer had been sent for us, his Grace exhibited considerable anxiety for our coming up; and then when he saw us crossing the fields at a gallop, and in so compact a body, he actually cried out, 'Ah! that's the way I like to see horse-artillery move.'"

25 *"Centre of the British Army at La Haye Sainte"*
From an engraving by T. Sutherland, 1816

27 *"A dismounted Life Guardsman fighting a Cuirassier whom he slew and made off with his horse"*

28 *"Captain Kelly of the Life Guards gallantly attacking a Cuirassier whom he slew"*

Both from Christopher Kelly "The Memorable Battle of Waterloo", 1817

26 *(overleaf)* *"The Battle of Waterloo"*
Drawn and engraved by John Burnett after J. A. Atkinson, with portraits by A. W. Devis, (1819)

squares, when I saw through the smoke the leading squadrons of the advancing column coming on at a brisk trot, and already not more than one hundred yards distant, if so much, for I don't think we could have seen so far. I immediately ordered the line to be formed for action—*case-shot!* and the leading gun was unlimbered and commenced firing almost as soon as the word was given: for activity and intelligence our men were unrivalled. The very first round, I saw, brought down several men and horses. They continued, however, to advance. I glanced at the Brunswickers, and that glance told me it would not do; they had opened a fire from their front faces, but both squares appeared too unsteady, and I resolved to say nothing about the Duke's order, and take our chance—a resolve that was strengthened by the effect of the remaining guns as they rapidly succeeded in coming into action, making terrible slaughter, and in an instant covering the ground with men and horses. Still they persevered in approaching us (the first round had brought them to a walk), though slowly, and it did seem they would ride over us. We were a little below the level of the ground on which they moved—having in front of us a bank of about a foot and a half or two feet high, along the top of which ran a narrow road—and this gave more effect to our case-shot, all of which almost must have taken effect, for the carnage was frightful."

A French soldier watched Mercer's men stand by the guns:

"Through the smoke I saw the English gunners abandon their pieces, all but six guns stationed under the road, and almost immediately our cuirassiers were upon the squares, whose fire was drawn in zig-zags. Now, I thought, those gunners would be cut to pieces; but no, the devils kept firing with grape, which mowed them down like grass."

"I suppose", continued Mercer,

"this state of things occupied but a few seconds, when I observed symptoms of hesitation, and in a twinkling, at the instant I thought it was all over with us, they turned to either flank and filed away rapidly to the rear. Retreat of the mass, however, was not so easy. Many facing about and trying to force their way through the body of the column, that part next to us became a complete mob, into which we kept a steady fire of case shot from our six pieces. The effect is hardly conceivable, and to paint this scene of slaughter and confusion impossible. Every discharge was accompanied by the fall of numbers, whilst the survivors struggled with each other, and I actually saw them using the pommels of their swords to fight their way out of the *mêlée*. Some, rendered desperate at finding themselves thus pent up at the muzzles of our guns, as it were, and others carried away by their horses, maddened with wounds, dashed through our intervals—few thinking of using their swords, but pushing furiously onward, intent only on saving themselves. At last the rear of the column, wheeling about, opened a passage, and the whole swept away at a much more rapid pace than they had advanced, nor stopped until the swell of the ground covered them from our fire. We then ceased firing; but as they were still not far off, for we saw the tops of their caps, having reloaded, we stood ready to receive them should they renew the attack.

"One of, if not the first man who fell on our side was wounded by his own gun. Gunner Butterworth was one of the greatest pickles in the troop, but, at the same time, a most daring, active soldier; he was No. 7 (the man who sponged, &c.) at his gun. He had just finished ramming down the shot, and was stepping back outside the wheel, when his foot stuck in the miry soil, pulling him forward at the moment the gun was fired. As a man naturally does when falling, he threw out both his arms before him, and they were blown off at the elbows. He raised himself a little on his two stumps, and looked up most piteously in my face. To assist him was impossible—the safety of all, everything, depended on our not slackening our fire, and I was obliged to turn from him. The state of anxious activity in which we were kept all day, and the numbers who fell almost immediately afterwards, caused me to lose sight of poor Butterworth; and I afterwards learned that he had succeeded in rising and was gone to the rear; but on inquiring for him next day, some of my people who had been sent to Waterloo told me that they saw his body lying by the roadside near the farm of Mont St. Jean—bled to death! The retreat of the cavalry was succeeded by a shower of shot and shells, which must have annihilated us had not the little bank covered and threw most of them over us. Still some reached us and knocked down men and horses."

"What was happening to the left and right of us", wrote Mercer,

"I know no more about than the man in the moon—not even what corps were beyond the Brunswickers. The smoke confined our vision to a very small compass, so that my battle was restricted to the two small squares and my own battery; and, as long as we maintained our ground, I thought it a matter of course that others did so too."

The batteries on either side had obeyed Wellington's instructions to retreat to the squares when the horsemen drew near. They were more fortunate in their neighbours than Mercer, who described the privates in the Brunswickers as being none of them older than eighteen, and all very frightened. His battery's success in defending their guns against extremely determined horsemen is a measure of their skill and courage, and of the senseless sacrifice Ney's folly inflicted on his cavalry. No doubt Mercer owed as much to luck as to resolution in not being overrun and having his guncrews cut down by the cuirassiers, for his guns were actually a little in advance of the rest of the English line. Although along the front conditions were anything but constant, it would not be fair to imagine that Mercer's battery, for all that they remained at their guns, had an easier time than most; at the end of the day there were more French killed and wounded before their position than any other.

Nearly all Wellington's guns had been captured and his squares surrounded by horsemen. From the Emperor's vantage point at Rossomme it seemed as if the mass of 5,000 cuirassiers which stretched along the slopes from Hougoumont to La Haye Sainte had broken the English line, as their forms were glimpsed through the smoke lapping the squares and occupying the battery positions. Yet the line stood intact as long as the squares held firm and the gunners remained safe inside them; to reach them the French cavalry had suffered appalling casualties—and for very little purpose. Their losses mounted as they rode around the English infantry, but the squares still failed to break. Wellington's soldiers soon came to welcome the presence of the cuirassiers, for they were not able to do much damage, and as long as they were there, the infantry knew that they would be spared the fire of the enemy artillery.

The history of the Waterloo Campaign is *par excellence* a record of lost chances, of opportunities squandered not singly, but in series. Ney had committed a terrible mistake in using cavalry when he did, but he could have reaped more profit from their sacrifice when they forced their way to the top of the ridge. The majority of the English batteries had been taken, and yet no attempt was made to silence the guns which made assault so murderous an affair. There were no horses or equipment to drag them away with. There were no spikes to make the guns useless. "It did not occur, even to a single officer", writes General Fuller, "to have the sponge-staves broken. Had the guns been spiked, which could have been done with headless nails and hammers, the next great cavalry assault would almost have certainly succeeded."

Lord Uxbridge had held his hand until the French squadrons were quite disrupted by their progress past and around the squares.

The horsemen were outnumbered and by now too disorganised to withstand the counter-attack; they broke, and made their escape as best they could, riding between the squares and through the volleys fired from them as they passed. Once in the shelter of the hollow below the English front, Milhaud's and Lefebvre-Desnouettes' Divisions formed up to return to the attack. The officers around the Emperor were exhilarated at the apparent success of the first charge, and began to think that the battle would soon be won when they saw their cavalry renew the assault so promptly, and reach the English squares and batteries yet again. Napoleon was less certain that Wellington's front was about to collapse.

For Mercer, the preliminary to the second attempt was:

" . . . a cloud of skirmishers, who galled us terribly by a fire of carbines and pistols at scarcely 40 yards from our front. We were obliged to stand with portfires lighted, so that it was not without a little difficulty that I succeeded in restraining our people from firing, for they grew impatient under such fatal results. Seeing some exertion beyond words necessary for this purpose, I leaped my horse up the little bank, and began a promenade (by no means agreeable) up and down our front, without ever drawing my sword, though these fellows were within speaking distance of me. This quietened my men; but the tall blue gentlemen, seeing me thus dare them, immediately made a target of me, and commenced a very deliberate practice, to show us what very bad shots they were and verify the old artillery proverb, 'The nearer the target, the safer you are.' One fellow certainly made me flinch, but it was a miss; so I shook my finger at him, and called him *coquin*, &c. The rogue grinned as he reloaded, and again took aim. I certainly felt rather foolish at that moment, but was ashamed, after such bravado, to let him see it, and therefore continued my promenade. As if to prolong my torment, he was a terrible time about it. To me it seemed an age. Whenever I turned, the muzzle of his infernal carbine still followed me. At length, bang it went, and whiz came the ball close to the back of my neck, and at the same instant down dropped the leading driver of one of my guns (Miller), into whose forehead the cursed missile had penetrated.

"The Column now once more mounted the plateau, and these popping gentry wheeled off right and left to clear the ground for their charge. The spectacle was imposing, and if ever the word sublime was appropriately applied it might surely be to it. On they came in compact squadrons, one behind the other, so numerous that those of the rear were still below the brow when the head of the column was but at some sixty or seventy yards from our guns. Their pace was a slow but steady trot. None of your furious but galloping charges was this, but a deliberate advance, at a deliberate pace, as of men resolved to carry their point. They moved in profound silence, and the only sound that could be heard from them amidst the incessant roar of battle was the low thunderlike reverberation of the ground beneath the simultaneous tread of so many horses. On our part was equal deliberation. Every man stood steadily at his post, the guns ready, loaded with a round shot first and a case over it; the tubes were in the vents; the port-fires glared and sputtered behind the wheels; and my word alone was wanting to hurl destruction on that goodly show of gallant men and noble horses. I delayed this, for experience had given me confidence. The Brunswickers partook of this feeling, and with their squares, much reduced in point of size—well closed, stood firmly, with arms at the recover, and eyes fixed on us, ready to commence their fire at our first discharge. It was indeed a grand and imposing spectacle! The column was led on this time by an officer in a rich uniform, his breast covered with decorations, whose earnest gesticulations were strangely contrasted with the solemn demeanour of those to whom they were addressed. I thus allowed them to advance unmolested until the head of the column might have been about fifty or sixty yards from us, and then gave the word, 'Fire!' The effect was terrible. Nearly the whole leading rank fell at once; and the round shot, penetrating the column, carried confusion throughout its extent. The ground, already encumbered with victims of the first struggle, became now almost impassable. Still, however, these devoted warriors struggled on, intent only on reaching us. The thing was impossible. Our guns were served with astonishing activity, whilst the running fire of the two squares was maintained with spirit. Those who pushed forward over the heaps of carcasses of men and horses gained but a few paces in advance, there to fall in their turn and add to the difficulties of those succeeding them. The discharge of every gun was followed by a fall of men and horses like that of grass before the mower's scythe. When the horse alone was killed, we could see the cuirassiers divesting themselves of the encumbrance and making their escape on foot. Still, for a moment, the confused mass (for all order was at an end) stood before us, vainly trying to urge their horses over the obstacles presented by their fallen comrades, in obedience to the now loud and rapid vociferations of him who had led them on and remained unhurt. As before, many cleared everything and rode through us; many came plunging forward only to fall, man and horse, close to the muzzles of our guns; but the majority again turned at the very moment when, from having less ground to go over, it were safer to advance than retire, and sought a passage to the rear. Of course the same confusion, struggle amongst themselves, and slaughter prevailed as before, until gradually they disappeared over the brow of the hill. We ceased firing, glad to take breath. Their retreat exposed us, as before, to a shower of shot and shells: these last, falling amongst us with very long fuses, kept burning and hissing a long time

149

before they burst, and were a considerable annoyance to man and horse. The bank in front, however, again stood our friend, and sent many over us innocuous."

Sergeant Morris was in the front face of the square of the 2nd Battalion of the 73rd Foot, and therefore witnessed the preparations for each successive cavalry charge. His battalion was one of the hardest hit, for it was the target for one of the few batteries which seconded the cavalry. Had Ney given them adequate artillery support it is difficult to see how the English squares could have continued to hold out. Morris's captain was aged sixty, and although he had spent 30 years in the army, had never been under fire until two days before, at Quatre Bras. Morris was in charge of the company's spirit ration, which he had drawn that morning.

"My comrade", he wrote,

"was on my right hand, in the front face of the square, in the front rank, kneeling; he had a trifling defect in his speech; at every charge the cavalry made, he would say 'Tom, Tom, here comes the *calvary*.'

"On their next advance they brought some artillery-men, turned the cannon in our front upon us, and fired into us with grape-shot, which proved very destructive, making complete lanes through us; and then the horsemen came to dash in at the openings. But before they reached, we had closed our files, throwing the dead outside, and taking the wounded inside the square; and they were forced again to retire. They did not, however, go further than the pieces of cannon—waiting there to try the effect of some more grapeshot. We saw the match applied, and again it came as thick as hail upon us. On looking round, I saw my left hand man falling backwards, the blood falling from his left eye; my poor comrade on the right, also by the same discharge, got a ball through his right thigh, of which he died a few days afterwards.

"Our situation, now, was truly awful; our men were falling by dozens at every fire. About this time, also, a large shell fell just in front of us, and while the fuze was burning out, we were wondering how many of us it would destroy. When it burst, about seventeen men were either killed or wounded by it; the portion which came to my share, was a piece of rough cast-iron, about the size of a horse-bean, which took up its lodging in my left cheek; the blood ran copiously down inside my clothes, and made me feel rather uncomfortable. Our poor captain was horribly frightened; and several times came to me for a drop of something to keep his spirits up. Towards the close of the day, he was cut in two by a cannon shot.

"The next charge the cavalry made, they deliberately walked

their horses up to the bayonet's point; and one of them, leaning over his horse, made a thrust at me with his sword. I could not avoid it, and involuntarily closed my eyes. When I opened them again, my enemy was lying just in front of me, within reach, in the act of thrusting at me. He had been wounded by one of my rear rank men, and whether it was the anguish of the wound, or the chagrin of being defeated, I know not; but he endeavoured to terminate his existence with his own sword; but that being too long for his purpose, he took one of our bayonets, which was lying on the ground, and raising himself up with one hand, he placed the point of the bayonet under his cuirass, and fell on it.

"The next time the cuirassiers made their appearance on our front, the Life Guards boldly rode out from our rear to meet them, and in point of numbers, they seemed pretty well matched. The French waited, with the utmost coolness, to receive them, opening their ranks to allow them to ride in.

"It was a fair fight, and the French were fairly beaten and driven off. I noticed one of the Guards, who was attacked by two cuirassiers, at the same time; he bravely maintained the unequal conflict for a minute or two, when he disposed of one of them by a deadly thrust in the throat. His combat with the other one lasted about five minutes, when the guardsman struck his opponent a slashing back-handed stroke, and sent his helmet some distance, with the head inside it. The horse galloped away, the headless rider sitting erect in the saddle, the blood spurting out of the arteries like so many fountains."

Napoleon watched the defeat of the second attack with mounting impatience. Ney had taken the majority of his cavalry and thrown them against unbroken infantry without even bothering to consult him. "This premature movement may produce fatal results", he told Soult. "Ney has compromised us as he did at Jena", replied the Chief of Staff.

The Emperor was in no doubt about the folly of committing so many horsemen in an unprepared assault, and it had been mounted on such a scale that he became worried about the effect its defeat might have on the army's morale. "This has taken place an hour too soon", he said to Soult, "but we must stand by what has been already done." There may have seemed little alternative to supporting Ney, but the situation on the slopes was not one to be redeemed merely by sending more cavalry to be slaughtered. Had artillery and infantry been ordered to accompany them, or even a number of field batteries by themselves, fresh horsemen might have won a quick break-through. Numbers alone would be of little use until the squares had been breached, and to employ more cavalry without withdrawing Milhaud's exhausted divisions would only overcrowd the front and blunt the edge of the assault. Nevertheless, Napoleon's orders ignored all such considerations; he simply told Flahaut, his aide-de-camp, to instruct Kellermann's two divisions and all the cavalry to support and follow Milhaud on the other side of the valley. Kellermann thought the order unwise, but he had no chance to dispute it with Flahaut because his first division was already moving off; its commander had started without waiting for Kellermann's confirmation. He accepted the *fait accompli* and set his own squadrons in motion. When he had reached a depression not far from Hougoumont, he halted one of his brigades, 800 carabiniers, and instructed the commander not to stir from the spot without his written order. Behind Kellermann's divisions followed a third, Guyot's Heavy Cavalry of the Guard. Whether or not the Emperor intended that this, his last mounted reserve, should join the struggle on the slopes, is rather obscure. It hardly seems likely that he would have wished to strip himself entirely of cavalry, yet Flahaut's vague but comprehensive order might well mean that the Guard should advance as well, and Guyot rode off without seeking any reassurance. The brigade Kellermann had detached from the assault on his own initiative were now Napoleon's sole cavalry reserve.

When the Emperor sent reinforcements to Milhaud the Prussians had begun to attack his right flank, and he was naturally prepared to accept almost any losses to defeat Wellington as quickly as possible, but this was not going to be done by flooding the field with still more horsemen. Above all, the cavalry needed room to manœuvre if they were to carry the allied lines by storm, and throwing fresh divisions into the assault made the task not less but more difficult. That Napoleon should have made such a mistake is almost incredible, and the first reaction of the English to the approaching assault was one of sheer astonishment. Before them there were now 9,000 cavalry preparing to attack the line between Hougoumont and La Haye Sainte, a distance of 1,000 yards, but because the French were obliged to avoid the zones of fire around the farm and the château they could only advance on a front of 500 yards.

29 *Wellington's reaction to Napoleon's order to use howitzers on Hougoumont (p. 136).* "*I see that the fire has communicated from the Haystack to the Roof of the Chateau. You must however still keep your Men in those parts to which the fire does not reach. Take care that no Men are lost by the falling in of the Roof, or floors. After they will have fallen in occupy the Ruined walls inside of the Garden; particularly if it should be possible for the Enemy to pass through the Embers in the Inside of the House.*"

30 *Wellington recalls his cavalry to meet Ney's massed cavalry assault of the mid-afternoon.* "*We ought to have more of the Cavalry between the two high Roads. That is to say, three Brigades at least, besides the Brigade in observation on the Right, & besides the Belgian Cavalry & the D. of Cumberland's Hussars. One heavy & one light Brigade might remain on the left.*"

Slips of prepared skin bearing pencilled orders by Wellington to his unit commanders

31, 32 *Obverse and reverse of the Waterloo medal*

33 *"La Belle Alliance": a plate from the porcelain service presented to Wellington by the King of Prussia*

Time was fast running out for the Emperor; a second battle was developing on his right flank, where the Prussian vanguard must be prevented from sweeping across his rear and his lines of communication. The English in front had to be in retreat before Blücher brought up all his forces, for if they were then still on the ridge there could be no hope of extricating the army from a struggle against an enemy twice its size and conducting a successful withdrawal. Accompanied by Blücher himself, Bülow's corps was the first to reach the battlefield, after an eleven hour march without food through appallingly difficult country. Joining Bülow at Chapelle-Saint-Lambert early that afternoon, Blücher decided that his best course would be to launch an attack on the Emperor's right flank, in the area of the village of Plancenoit. From Chapelle-Saint-Lambert the road they followed descends a steep valley to a stream called the Lasne after which it climbs just as abruptly to the top of the opposite slope. Even in dry weather the route seems almost impassable to artillery, and it is surprising that Blücher's guns were able to make the journey over sodden ground. Blücher was determined to honour his promise to Wellington, and rode along the column encouraging his struggling and exhausted troops. "Now then, comrades," he said to a battery he met straining at the wheels of a cannon which had become bogged down in heavy mud, "surely you would not have me break my word."

It was half-past four when Bülow's leading divisions opened fire on the French cavalry posted before them. In such a situation attack was the only form of defence; the French were outnumbered three to one, and there was no room for defensive manœuvre. Domon's cavalry charged the hussars of the Prussian advanced guard only to be halted by the fire of the infantry and artillery coming up behind them. The French squadrons broke off the engagement, wheeling away to reveal Lobau's advancing regiments. Lobau saw that it would be fatal to attempt to stand his ground; he was faced by superior forces which were increasing with every minute that passed, and he could not retreat very far without endangering the whole of the French right. He decided to attack before Bülow could deploy the rest of his divisions. Lobau's seasoned troops drove the enemy back and forced them to continue their retreat until two more divisions came up to support them.

Although they were now outnumbered by three to one the French succeeded in holding their new positions. Blücher did not waste time and men attempting to recapture them, but switched his attack to Plancenoit to threaten Lobau's right. The French were obliged to abandon their ground and send a brigade to hold the village. The defenders were promptly forced out of Plancenoit by sheer weight of numbers. The assault was still taking place when Blücher received a despatch from Thielmann, announcing that he was being attacked at Wavre by Grouchy's superior force, and doubting whether he could hold them off on his own. "Let Thielmann defend himself as best he can", said Gneisenau, the Prussian Chief of Staff, "it scarcely matters if he is crushed at Wavre providing we can gain the victory here."

The Emperor's situation was rapidly deteriorating; should another Prussian corps come up to join Wellington in front of him or Bülow on his right before the English were defeated, the scales would be turned and his army would be struggling for its existence. Meanwhile he did what he could to meet his fresh difficulties. As Lobau went forward to attack the Prussians he instructed Durutte to intensify the assault on Papelotte and La Haye in order to assist Ney's offensive along the centre and to cut the communications between Bülow's right and Wellington's left. Lobau's troops were unable to withstand the numbers sent against them, and with the fall of Plancenoit the Prussian artillery were in range of the centre of the battlefield; shells began to fall near the Emperor and his staff and struck the battalions of the Guard standing in reserve. Napoleon ordered Duhesme to attack the village with his division of the Young Guard, and for a while his success there relieved the pressure on the French right flank.

Between five and half-past Ney accomplished the ruin of the Emperor's magnificent divisions of cavalry, the strongest arm of his army. Still blind to the uselessness of using cavalry without proper support, despite the experiences of the last two hours, Ney mustered the last regiments he could find until he had packed 9,000 horsemen into an area in which there was not room for more than a thousand to manœuvre. The squadrons were so crowded together that the pressure forced horses and riders from the ground. With no help from their infantry, and little from their guns, the cavalry rode slowly forward to meet all three arms. Ney led them to sacrifice without victory; no price could purchase success on these terms. The cuirassiers threw away their scabbards as sign of their determination not to sheath their swords again; each time they were driven away from the squares they made their way back once more, past the dead and dying who encumbered the slopes in mounting numbers, through volleys of musketry and salvoes of grapeshot. "The French cavalry made some of the boldest charges I ever saw", said Frazer, "they sounded the whole extent of our line. . . . Never did cavalry behave so nobly, or was received by infantry so firmly." The squares were almost invulnerable to cavalry alone, and yet Ney left whole regiments of infantry standing idle all day watching the struggle on the slopes. Although there was an abundance of artillery waiting to be used, "only one battery was brought up in the rear of the horsemen to breach the allied squares", writes General Fuller. "Undoubtedly, the heavy, churned-up ground made artillery movement difficult; nevertheless, had but two or three horse-artillery batteries been advanced to within case-shot range, nothing could have saved Wellington's army."

"This time", said Mercer of the renewed assault, "it was child's play. They could not even approach us in decent order, and we fired most deliberately; it was folly having attempted the thing." The confusion was pitiful: the fresh regiments lost their cohesion as they jostled for space with the tired survivors of the earlier attacks; riderless horses strayed over the field; the walking wounded threw away their armour to speed their escape. Those who reached the allied lines fought with a desperation that came from the hopelessness of the task. Ney, whose third horse had been killed under him, was seen standing by an abandoned English battery, furiously striking the mouth of a cannon with the blade of his sword; in him, as in his men, rage and frustration had supplanted reason. He took another horse, and more men, and led them again to the assault, but no effort, however heroic, could controvert the logic of elementary tactics. Repulsed again and again by the fusillades from the squares, and the counter-attacks of Wellington's cavalry, themselves as exhausted as their opponents, the French withdrew from the inferno at the top of the slopes; "it was like being at the door of a hot oven", declared one witness.

Some of the French squadrons preferred to ride beyond the squares and return by detours rather than expose themselves to the fire of the infantry as they retreated. Sergeant Wheeler's company, posted on the far right of the English front, intercepted some escaping cuirassiers.

> " . . . In one of these [cavalry] charges made by the enemy a great many overcharged themselves and could not get back without exposing themselves to the deadly fire of the infantry. Not choosing to return by the way they came they took a circuitous route and came down the road on our left. There were nearly one hundred of them, all Cuirassiers. Down they rode full gallop, the trees thrown across the bridge on our left stopped them. We saw them coming and was prepared, we opened our fire, the work was done in an instant. By the time we had loaded and the smoke had cleared away, one and only one, solitary individual was seen running over the brow in our front. One other was saved by Capt. Jno. Ross from being put to death by some of the Brunswickers.
> "I went to see what effect our fire had had, and never before beheld such a sight in so short a space, as about an hundred men and horses could be huddled together there they lay. Those who were shot dead were fortunate for the wounded horses in their struggles by plunging and kicking so finished what we had begun. In examining the men we could not find one that would be like to recover, and as we had other business to attend to we were obliged to leave them to their fate."

Only when the last cavalry attack ended did Ney use the 6,000 infantry who had waited all afternoon less than a mile from the English front. They could have been brought up under the cover of the cavalry charges without suffering many casualties, for most of the allied batteries were abandoned at each advance the cavalry had made; and once in the firing line, Wellington's squares would have been no match for fresh troops attacking in open order. When they did at last go forward, they were quite unsupported, the English artillerymen returned to their guns, the English infantry were free from the threat of a cavalry charge, and within minutes of approaching the ridge, Ney's troops were driven back with a loss of 1,500 killed, wounded and scattered.

Ney had been instructed to take La Haye Sainte before he became side-tracked into mounting the first cavalry assault. Since then he had made several further attacks with cavalry, and finally one with infantry, and still showed no sign of preparing to capture La Haye Sainte. The farm and sand pit were the key to any successful attempt to storm the English centre; from them his artillery would be able to reply to Wellington's, and blast gaps in the allied line through which he could push the infantry. At last the Emperor sent orders that La Haye Sainte was to be taken at any cost. Fighting had continued there throughout the afternoon, but with less sense of urgency than elsewhere, and with no result. The defenders had begun to run short of ammunition, and Wellington had none to send.

8

Waterloo: Evening

NEY DIRECTED THE ATTACK on La Haye Sainte with undeterred enthusiasm. He assembled a regiment of infantry and a
detachment of engineers, and sent them to storm the walls of the
farm, which fell only after violent resistance. Volleys of point-blank
musket fire brought down many of the assailants before they
reached the buildings, but others rushed forward, seizing the
musket barrels protruding from the loopholes, and clambering on
the heaps of dead, scaled the walls from which they shot at the
outnumbered Germans in the courtyard below. Some of the engineers battered at the door with an axe which passed from hand to
hand as the users were shot, until the door gave way and the
French rushed into the yard. The defenders had spent their ammunition, and made their last stand with side-arms. Only Major Baring
and 42 men of the nine companies which had been posted in the
farm were able to make their escape through the besiegers and
return to the English lines.

Ney's success in this long-postponed operation transformed the
situation in the allied lines. He was now able to bring up a battery
of horse artillery to a mound close to the farm buildings, and at a
range of less than 300 yards these few guns wrought havoc along
the English centre. With the loss of the farm the sand pit had to
be abandoned as well, leaving the French skirmishers in excellent
cover only 80 yards from Wellington's line, on which they began
to pour a heavy and accurate fire. The decisive hour of the battle
had arrived. The survivors of Allix, Donzelot and Marcognet's
divisions, which had taken part in the first great assault, now
advanced under the cover of the *tirailleurs* and the horse battery
towards the weakening allied centre. They reached the road along

the ridge where they began a desperate struggle at bayonet-point for the possession of the hedges and banks. The pressure continued to mount along the English front, and Wellington's reserves were almost exhausted. His line retained its strength only as long as it was not breached at any point; if this were to happen when there were no reserves immediately at hand to drive them off, the enemy could widen the breach and deepen their penetration before reinforcements could be brought up from quieter stretches of the front, providing, of course, they still had enough troops left to push through the gap. The defenders on either side of the break-through would become frightened of being outflanked, and would fall back to save themselves, freeing more men to exploit the advantage. The defence would collapse quickly: communications would be severed, ammunition and baggage parks captured, and the army scattered in a disordered retreat. Ney's thrust on either side of La Haye Sainte was threatening to develop into just such a situation.

Colonel Ompteda led two battalions of the German Legion down the main road in a counter-attack towards the farm. He achieved an initial success, but very soon his troops were halted by the weight of the numbers in front of them. The rear battalion came under very heavy fire, before which they retreated as Ompteda was struck and fell dying from his horse. The battalion in front, drawn up in open order, was overwhelmed by a squadron of cuirassiers, and only 30 survived the charge. Formations were melting away in Wellington's centre; the remains of Ompteda's brigade were incapable of continued resistance, Kielmansegge's retreated to the rear of Mont-Saint-Jean, Kruse's dissolved before its commander's eyes. Headed by their Colonel, the entire regiment of the Cumberland Hussars turned and rode away towards Brussels. The only cavalry remaining near the centre, Somerset and Ponsonby's brigades, were reduced to a couple of squadrons deployed in single file to make their numbers seem greater. Casualties mounted amongst the senior officers; the Prince of Orange and General Alten were both wounded and forced to retire; two of Wellington's aides-de-camp were killed. The streams of wounded men leaving the firing line were swelled by comrades making their own escape on the pretext of helping them.

So heavy were the losses and the desertions that the centre of Wellington's line was left open. "We were in peril", wrote Kennedy, "at every moment the issue of the battle became more than doubtful." Away to his left the Duke's front was firmly held, but on the extreme left, Durutte had taken Papelotte for the second time. On the right, between La Haye Sainte and Hougoumont, where bitter fighting still continued, the allied troops were exhausted from the successive cannonades and cavalry charges of the afternoon. The French were no less tired, no less depleted in numbers, but a small number of men, a further thrust at the centre, one last effort, might be sufficient to topple Wellington's army into a chaotic rout. The Duke could see Bülow's corps attacking Napoleon's flank away in the distance, but none of the Prussians had yet joined him on the ridge. He had despatched several aides-de-camp down the dangerous road to Ohain to hasten Zieten's corps to his assistance, but for the moment, there was nothing he could do to relieve the danger to his centre. Officers came up continually to ask for help, reporting their situation as desperate, and seeking fresh orders; he could say nothing to them except to stand in their positions and fight to the last man.

Ney had seen wavering in the English line, and the withdrawal of hardpressed regiments to fresh positions; he noticed the crowds of wounded and fugitives going to the rear, and the thinness of the lines they had left. All would have been redeemed, victory would yet have been his, if he had still had in reserve a few of the thousands of troops spent in fruitless assaults throughout the afternoon. Little more could be done with the men who had so shaken Wellington's centre; they had made their effort. He needed only a few fresh troops to reap the profit of their sacrifice and brush aside the exhausted allied army. He sent Colonel Heymès to ask the Emperor for a small infantry reinforcement. "Troops!" exclaimed Napoleon, "where do you expect me to get them? Do you expect me to make them?" The Emperor refused. He had the men, fourteen battalions of his best infantry: eight of the Old and six of the Middle Guard. If he had been prepared to accept this last small raise in the stakes, he must have pierced Wellington's front and defeated his army. In his earlier days Napoleon would have sent up the Guard, overwhelmed Wellington's broken regiments, and regained the initiative to such an extent that not only would the English be routed and Brussels abandoned but the Prussians would also be obliged to retreat in order to concentrate their scattered corps.

When Heymès came up with his message Napoleon had been preoccupied by the renewed threat to his right flank, where the Prussians had driven Duhesme's battalions of the Young Guard out of Plancenoit. It has been suggested that he was too concerned by the danger of a Prussian outbreak across his rear to pay much attention to Ney's request. Alternatively it is argued that the Emperor was anxious to keep some of the Guard out of the battle now that Ney's use of the cavalry of the Guard had robbed him of his usual reserve. Neither of these hypotheses meets the facts. The Emperor must have realised that if the battle were not won in the ninety minutes before nightfall, he was bound to lose his army, the campaign and his throne. The situation was indivisible although it extended over two fronts; he had to hold the Prussians back *and* defeat Wellington, and if he could not the battle was lost. Moreover, both tasks had to be accomplished at once. It made no difference that while his troops were being pushed back by the Prussians, Ney's were more than holding their own; the position was as critical on one front as on the other; Ney's chances of success were diminishing with every minute that passed. Now was the time to commit all the remaining reserves, without thinking of hoarding a few battalions to meet another emergency, for if either the Prussians continued to advance or Ney failed to overcome the English line in the next quarter of an hour, the situation would be far beyond redemption.

Napoleon cannot have left Ney unsupported for half an hour because he did not recognise the need to reinforce the assault, and the reasons for his delay must remain a mystery. It has been advanced that the Emperor was overcome by physical exhaustion, but this view can be discounted on a number of grounds. His fits of lethargy during the Waterloo Campaign were more the symptom than the cause of his mistakes. Possibly he no longer had the will to execute what his mind must have told him was the sole course he could follow. It is by no means rare to find a general's will to wage war desert him while his strength and skill are still largely unimpaired; and although there was certainly no falling off in the Emperor's strategy in 1815, once away from his maps and engaged on the battlefield, he was no longer the commander of Italy and Austerlitz. He had prophesied as much ten years before, at Austerlitz: "Ordener* is worn out. One has but a short time for war. I am good for another six years, and then I shall have to stop."†

Two battalions of the Old Guard were sent to recover Plancenoit, where they gave an astonishing demonstration of the worth of seasoned troops. Passing the disorganised Young Guard, whom Duhesme was trying to rally in front of the village, and dispensing altogether with musket fire, they entered Plancenoit at the charge, driving the enemy out with their bayonets. They pursued the Prussians 600 yards beyond the village and overran their batteries. Behind them the Young Guard marched back into Plancenoit, and as they did so, Lobau regained some of the ground to their left.

Satisfied that his flank was now secure, a little after seven o'clock the Emperor turned his attention again to the situation of his main front. Wellington still seemed to be on the point of defeat; the French had enveloped Hougoumont on his right, and had advanced beyond the Nivelles road which runs behind the château; the exhausted regiments in his centre continued to struggle with the troops who had reached the road along the ridge; and on his far left Papelotte remained in the hands of the enemy. Napoleon decided to send the Guard to carry the English front, but although he issued his orders only a few minutes after the recapture of Plancenoit, by the time the column had been brought into action, Wellington had been given a half-hour's respite in which to re-organise his defences, and more important still, Zieten had come up on his left, releasing troops to reinforce the centre of the line, and threatening the Emperor's right wing into the bargain. The issue of the battle, however, had hung by an even slenderer thread than the passage of thirty minutes. Zieten had been delayed at several points on his route to the battlefield, and when his advanced guard reached Ohain at six o'clock, the majority of his troops were still some distance away.

* One of his generals.
† Six years after Austerlitz Napoleon was preparing to invade Russia.

Here Zieten was met by Colonel Freemantle, one of the aides-de-camp the Duke had sent to hasten his approach. The aide explained how desperate the situation had become, and asked for immediate help, if only to the extent of 3,000 men. Zieten was fearful of committing his corps piecemeal lest they should be defeated in detail, and told Colonel Freemantle that he would come to the Duke's assistance once the rest of his force had caught up with him. While Zieten waited to continue his march he despatched an officer to reconnoitre the approaches through which he would pass to join the English. The officer came back with the alarming news that the allied army was in full retreat from Mont-Saint-Jean; he had been deceived by the large numbers of wounded and fugitives leaving the front line. Convinced that his fears had been more than justified, Zieten turned his troops to the left to support Bülow in his struggle with Lobau and the Young Guard. Fortunately for Wellington, Müffling, the Prussian general attached to his staff, had ridden to the heights above Papelotte to watch Zieten enter the English line, and when he saw him turn away to join Bülow he galloped up to the retreating corps. Zieten was unwilling to change his direction again, but Müffling was insistent: "The battle is lost", he said, "if the first corps does not go to the Duke's rescue." Much against his will, Zieten was at last persuaded to counter-march his troops.

The battalions of the Imperial Guard were still making their way to La Haye Sainte to begin their assault when Zieten's column appeared from Smohain, and headed for the junction of the two French fronts. The sight of a fresh body of the enemy bearing down on them was too much for some of the Emperor's exhausted and disheartened infantry, and they began to retreat until Napoleon rode up to them and persuaded them to return to their positions.

If the Guard had been sent forward when Ney asked for reinforcements, they would have found it a simple matter to come up under the cover of the troops already on the ridge and make their way through the remains of Wellington's centre, already engaged with the débris of d'Erlon's corps. By the time they did arrive, the situation had changed out of all recognition. Wellington had called in fresh troops from his right and left, and these, with the brigades already on the spot, cleared the ridge of the French who had held it for so long. Unharassed by skirmishers, the allied batteries were able to resume their fire, quickly silencing the battery at La Haye Sainte which had done such damage to the centre of the English line. The Guard were left to deliver their assault without the support of close artillery and musket fire, and as they approached, the defenders were strengthened by the arrival of Chassé's division of Dutch-Belgian infantry, and six fresh regiments of cavalry under Vivian and Vandeleur which had been relieved above Papelotte by Zieten's arrival.

The French artillery were ordered to increase their bombardment of the front, but Wellington's precautions continued to rob the shelling of much of its effect:

> "The regiment", wrote Ensign Leeke of the 52nd, "stood about forty paces below the crest of the position, so that it was nearly or quite out of fire. The roar of round-shot still continued, many only just clearing our heads—others striking the top of our position and bounding over us—others again, almost spent and rolling down gently towards us. One of these, when we were standing in line, came rolling down like a cricket ball, so slowly that I was putting out my foot to stop it, when my colour-sergeant quickly begged me not to do so, and told me that it might have seriously injured my foot. Exactly in front of me, when standing in line, lay, at the distance of two yards, a dead tortoise-shell kitten. It had probably been frightened out of Hougoumont, which was the nearest house to us, and about a quarter of a mile off.
>
> "There was a peculiar smell at this time, arising from a mingling of the smell of the wheat trodden down flat with the smell of gunpowder."

The battalions of the Guard chosen for the attack were being drawn up across the valley when an officer of the carabiniers rode up to the skirmishers of Leeke's regiment holding his sheathed sword high above him, and shouting "Vive le Roi!" He had intended to desert earlier in the day, but had delayed in the hope that he could induce some of his comrades to join him. "Get ready!" he cried, "that scoundrel Napoleon will be upon you with his Guard in less than half an hour." The information was forwarded to Wellington, who rode along his line from the elm tree above La Haye Sainte to the far right above Hougoumont, supervising the deployment of the reinforcements he brought up to meet the Guard's attack. The Emperor sent General de la Bédoyère with a number of officers along the whole of the front to announce Grouchy's arrival. The ingenuous Ney protested at the spreading of such a falsehood, but it served to hearten the troops whose morale had been shaken by the appearance of Zieten's corps. Napoleon intended to support the Guard with a general advance, but the order was not obeyed along most of the front and where it was, evoked only a feeble response; the five battalions of the Imperial Guard marched forward alone to storm the allied positions.

The exact circumstances of this, the most celebrated passage of arms in the Napoleonic Wars, have been in dispute ever since it occurred. From Ney downwards the witnesses have given conflicting accounts of the number of battalions taking part, of the formation in which they attacked, and the regiments they fought. The English First Foot Guards were given the title of Grenadiers in recognition of their defeat of the grenadiers of the Imperial Guard, although in actual fact it was the *chasseurs*, and not the *grenadiers*, who attacked them. An absurd and heated controversy arose as to which regiment was responsible for the repulse of the Guard, although the French came up at a number of points along the English front. The witnesses were, of course, too concerned with what was going on around them to pay much attention to what was happening elsewhere, and because of the dense smoke hanging over the line, visibility was rarely more than eighty to a hundred yards. When the Guard was delivering its assault, Mercer was too preoccupied with the shelling his battery had received to be aware that the last great struggle of the day was taking place. On another part of the front, Kincaid of the Rifle Brigade had so restricted a view of the battle that he did not realise at first that the Guard had been repulsed and that Wellington had ordered a general advance. Mistaken reports were inevitable in such conditions and it is hardly surprising that there should have been such confusion about the precise details of the Emperor's last offensive.

Shortly after the news of Grouchy's arrival had been spread along the front, the Emperor's troops caught sight of the Guard approaching La Haye Sainte by the Brussels road. Its appearance on the front had been so often the prelude of victory that even the wounded lying by the roadside raised themselves to shout encouragements as the veterans went by. Six hundred yards from the

English lines Napoleon handed the Guard over to Ney, and as the first battalion passed the Emperor standing between two batteries in the middle of the road, they gave him a last and tremendous salute. The battalions marched towards the enemy in review order, drawn up in ranks 75 to 80 wide, their arms at the present, and the officers in front, swords drawn. Two eight pounders accompanied each battalion, firing as they advanced. By the side of the leading troops rode Ney, until his horse was shot under him for the fifth time that day; he disentangled himself and continued his march on foot.

Although considerable confusion has arisen over the number of the Guard taking part in the attack, there is little reason to doubt that six battalions joined Napoleon at La Haye Sainte, one of which he placed in reserve well behind the others, leaving Ney to lead five in the actual assault, and not four, or eight as many accounts suggest. No explanation has ever been offered for the Marshal's strange choice of route to the allied lines. The obvious approach was by way of the Brussels road, as being the shortest distance the Guard would have to march under fire; it ran, moreover, through cuttings which offered good cover against the English artillery. Instead, Ney left the road, and struck to the left in a path which took his men farther than they need have gone, across the uneven and unprotected slopes covered by the dead and wounded of the great cavalry attacks of the afternoon. Marching in haste, for the Emperor had hurried on the assault when he heard of Zieten's threat to his right wing, the column of battalions broke in two as they made their way through the clouds of smoke which lay over the field. The rear half inclined more to the left than the one in front, and by the time the second column reached the enemy the first had already been defeated. "The drummers were beating the *pas de charge*", wrote Ensign Leeke, of the minutes which passed before the French appeared in front of his regiment, "which sounded as well as I can recollect, very much like this, 'the rum dum, the rum dum, the rummadum dummadum, dum, dum,' then '*Vive l'Empereur!*' This was repeated again and again (for) about a quarter of an hour or twenty minutes."

Two hundred yards from the allied positions the Guard came under the fire of 30 guns drawn up in a long curve along the slopes from the north of Hougoumont to the cross roads above La Haye Sainte. At every salvo the double charges of grapeshot swept away files in each battalion, but the Guard closed their ranks and continued to march at an even pace, still shouting "*Vive l'Empereur!*". The first troops to close with the English were the 1st Battalion of the Third Regiment of Grenadiers. They overran some Brunswickers who stood in their path and seized two English batteries. Next they attacked the left-hand square of Halkett's brigade, formed by the 30th and 73rd Regiments of Foot, and drove them back in confusion. Friant was wounded about this time, and made his way back to the French lines convinced that the battle was virtually won; but a single battalion, even of the Guard, stood no chance against the numbers about to attack them. General Chassé* brought up a battery of horse artillery to fire grapeshot into the Grenadiers' left flank, and then sent Ditmer's 3,000 men in a bayonet charge against their right, which swept the remains of the battalion to the bottom of the slopes. The 4th Grenadiers of the Imperial Guard had assaulted the right-hand square of Halkett's brigade, the 33rd and 69th Regiments, which began to give way under their musket fire and the shelling of the two eight pounders they had brought with them. General Halkett took the standard of the 33rd to encourage his men to hold their ground, and although he soon fell seriously wounded, he had succeeded in halting their retreat.

Wellington himself was standing close behind them when the English First Foot Guards were attacked by the 1st and 2nd Battalions of the 3rd Regiment of *Chasseurs*. The preliminary cannonade was unusually heavy, and the Foot Guards took shelter behind the banks of the road along the ridge. "Without the protection of this bank every creature must have perished", wrote Captain Powell in his journal.

> "Suddenly the firing ceased, and as the smoke cleared away a most superb sight opened on us. A close column of Grenadiers (*sic*) . . . were seen ascending the rise *au pas de charge* shouting *Vive l'Empereur!* They continued to advance till about 50 or 60 yards of our front, when the Brigade were ordered to stand up."

* The Belgian General Chassé had distinguished himself fighting for the Emperor a year before at Arcis-sur-Aube.

It was the Duke who gave the command; "Up Guards, ready." "Whether", continues Powell,

"it was from the sudden and unexpected appearance of a Corps so near them, which must have seemed as starting out of the ground, or the tremendously heavy fire we threw into them, *La Garde*, who had never before failed in an attack *suddenly* stopped. . . . In less than a minute about 300 were down. They now wavered, and several of the rear divisions began to draw out as if to deploy."

The French ranks had been shattered by the volleys of musket fire, and their path was obstructed by the heaps of dead and wounded around them. Despite their confusion, their only chance of success lay in pressing forward immediately, while they retained a little of the initiative. Instead, the officers of the *Chasseurs* made the mistake of trying to deploy their men in line to meet fire with fire. The English continued their fusillade as the Imperial Guard struggled to reform, and the French became only more confused. Those in the rear began to fire wildly over the heads of their comrades in front, minutes passed without closing with the enemy or forming lines to return their fire. Seeing the enemy waver, Wellington ordered the charge. The *Chasseurs* were too disordered and too few to resist and were pursued in a furious hand to hand struggle down to the orchard at Hougoumont. "The combatants were so mingled together", wrote one of the gunners, "that we had to stop firing."

The pursuit was abruptly called off. The battalion of the 4th Chasseurs, the last of Ney's assault column, were advancing to the support of the *Chasseurs* as well as the 4th *Grenadiers* who were withdrawing from their encounter with Halkett's righthand square. Maitland's Foot Guards returned hurriedly to their positions at the top of the slope, closely followed by the French. The 4th *Chasseurs* reached Wellington's line and attacked the Guards and the remains of Halkett's brigade. Until now, Ensign Leeke's regiment, the 52nd Light Infantry, had been concealed behind the reverse slope, but when their commander, Sir John Colborne, saw the leading *Chasseurs* pass by less than a hundred yards away, he brought the regiment forward over the crest of the ridge, and deployed his men in line along the enemy's left flank. At such a range their massed fire caused enormous casualties, to which the *Chasseurs* were unable to reply effectively. No troops, however

34 "*View of the Village of Waterloo, the day after the Battle*" (*Note the Horse Artillery in the foreground, p. 32*)

From an engraving by T. Sutherland, 1816

35 "View from Mont St Jean . . at the commencement of the grand charge made on the French . . . on the evening of the 18th June . . . "

From R. Bowyer, "The Campaign of Waterloo", 1816

seasoned, could withstand such losses, and they fled before the charge which followed towards the Brussels road on their right, carrying with them the troops in their path. For the troops along the Emperor's front the shouts of "*La Garde recule!*" were the signal that the battle was lost; a wholesale withdrawal began.

At the foot of the slopes the infantry and cavalry which had begun to march at last to the support of the Guard stopped in their tracks at the sight of the Guard itself in retreat. Above La Haye Sainte, Allix and Donzelot's divisions were still struggling with the allied infantry when they saw the Guard falling back in disorder on the road which ran through their front; as they too withdrew down the hill they brought Marcognet's division with them. Farther still to the right, at Papelotte and La Haye, Durutte's infantry were attacked by the Prussians, who had now concentrated overwhelming numbers of fresh troops. It was from this extreme wing of the battle that the retreat became a rout. Having been assured that the forces massing on their right were Grouchy's, the French were seized by panic when they discovered the truth: "*Nous sommes trahis!*" they cried, "*Sauve qui peut!*" No more was needed to transform a tired attack into a headlong rush for the rear. When Papelotte fell d'Erlon's corps abandoned the whole of the Emperor's right front. On the left the retreat of the Guard destroyed all order, and the masses of men who occupied the valley were no longer able to defend themselves.

Hardly fifteen minutes after the retreat of the last battalion of the Guard, Wellington rode to the edge of the plateau, took off his hat, and waved it in the air as the signal for a general advance. Every formation in a condition to march forward joined in the attack. In the van of the allied army Vivian and Vandeleur's cavalry poured exultantly down the slopes. "I have seen nothing like that moment", wrote Frazer,

> "the sky literally darkened with smoke, the sun just going down, and which had not for some hours broken through the gloom of the day, the indescribable shouts of thousands, where it was impossible to distinguish between friend and foe. Every man's arm seemed to be raised against that of every other. Suddenly, after the mingled mass had ebbed and flowed, the enemy began to yield; and cheerings and English huzzas announced that the day must be ours."

Away on the left of the English line, Kincaid and his men heard the cheering accompanying the general advance, which they were unable to see for the clouds of white smoke which hemmed them in. Guessing what had happened, they too went forward some minutes after the French had begun to retreat. "This movement", wrote Kincaid,

> "had carried us clear of the smoke; and, to people who had been for so many minutes enveloped in darkness, in the midst of destruction, and naturally anxious about the result of the day, the scene which now met the eye conveyed a feeling of more exquisite gratification than can be conceived. It was a fine summer's evening, just before sunset. The French were flying in one confused mass. British lines were seen in close pursuit, and in admirable order, as far as the eye could reach to the right, while the plain to the left was filled with Prussians."

One of the units unable to join in the rout of the Emperor's army was Mercer's battery, which had come under the misdirected fire of some Prussian guns—a further reminder of the confusion caused by the dense smoke and restricted area of the Napoleonic battlefield.

> "My recollections of the latter part of his day are rather confused; I recollect clearly, however, that we had ceased firing—the plain below being covered with masses of troops, which we could not distinguish from each other. Captain Walcot of the horse-artillery—had come to us, and we were all looking out anxiously at the movements below and on the opposite ridge, when he suddenly shouted out, 'Victory!—victory! they fly!—they fly!' and sure enough we saw some of the masses dissolving, as it were, and those composing them streaming away in confused crowds over the field, whilst the already desultory fire of their artillery ceased altogether. I shall never forget this joyful moment!—this moment of exultation! On looking round I found we were left almost alone. Cavalry and infantry had all moved forward, and only a few guns here and there were to be seen on the position. . . . We were congratulating ourselves on the happy results of the day, when an aide-de-camp rode up, crying 'Forward, sir!—forward! It is of the utmost importance that this movement should be supported by artillery!' At the same time waving his hat much in the manner of a huntsman laying on his dogs. I smiled at his energy, and pointing to the remains of my poor troop, quietly asked, 'How, sir?' A glance was sufficient to show him the impossibility, and away he went. Our situation was indeed terrible: of 200 fine horses with which we had entered the battle, upwards of 140 lay dead, dying, or severely wounded. Of the men, scarcely two-thirds of those necessary for four guns remained, and these so completely exhausted as to be totally incapable of further exertion. . . . My poor men, such at least as were

174

untouched, fairly worn out, their clothes, faces, &c. blackened by the smoke and spattered over with mud and blood, had seated themselves on the trails of the carriages, or had thrown themselves on the wet and polluted soil, too fatigued to think of anything but gaining a little rest. . . . For myself, I was also excessively tired—hoarse, to making speech painful, and deaf from the infernal uproar of the last eleven hours. Moreover, I was devoured by a burning thirst, not a drop of liquid having passed my lips since the evening of the 16th; but although, with the exception of the chicken's leg last night, I may be said to have eaten nothing for two whole days, yet did I not feel the least desire for food."

Napoleon was standing at La Haye Sainte busily engaged in forming a fresh assault column of three battalions of the Old Guard when he saw the whole of his left front give way. He quickly broke up the column into three squares, placing the right hand one across the Brussels road, in the hope that the fugitives might rally behind them, and march away in an orderly retreat. 1,500 men were too few to beat off a general offensive. Vivian's hussars hardly paused to waste time and men attacking squares when richer pickings lay around them on every side, and they rode on into the hordes of disorganised troops, sabring almost at will, and causing fresh panic. Behind them galloped the remains of Wellington's cavalry, sweeping aside the Emperor's last horsemen, the four *escadrons de service* which he had sent forward in a desperate attempt to halt their advance. The squares were raked by close artillery fire, and then attacked by long lines of infantry. At last the Emperor gave the Guard the order to retreat, and they fell back surrounded by infantry and cavalry in overwhelming numbers. Slowly, and with admirable courage, the squares cut their way through the enemy and the fugitives, pausing every few minutes to reform their ranks and repel fresh attacks. When they had lost too many men to maintain the three rank square formation, they arranged themselves in triangles two ranks deep and continued their march through the mêlée until they regained the plateau in the rear of the French position. A few minutes from the end, the English called on them to surrender, to which Cambronne, their commander, replied with one word: *"Merde!"** The

* The phrase, *"La garde meurt, mais ne se rend pas!"* was not Cambronne's, but a Paris journalist's. "The Duke", writes Maxwell, his biographer, "used to add that there was a set of ladies at Brussels, partisans of the Prince of Orange, called *la vieille garde*, of whom it is said, '*Elles ne meurent pas et se rendent toujours.*'"

survivors of the three squares were not long on the plateau before they were swamped by the simultaneous attacks of the English and Prussian infantry and cavalry.

With the destruction of the squares the last organised resistance on the battlefield came to an end. Unimaginable confusion reigned around La Belle Alliance where the bulk of the Emperor's army had been driven by the converging English and Prussian offensives. Lobau's front collapsed before Bülow's corps as the Guard delivered the last assault on Wellington's lines, and his men were swept back into the flank of the thousands fleeing before the English together with Durutte's division which had been thrown out of Papelotte. The two allied armies closed in on the vast mass of fugitives. Fired upon from all sides, pressed back by bayonet charges, and harried by thousands of cavalry, the French struggled helplessly towards the overcrowded roads leading from the field. Terrified by the shouts of the men falling behind them, the crowds surged onwards, leaving in their wake a débris of deserted baggage and artillery, arms and equipment of all kinds, and men trampled to death. The sun had now set, and darkness brought new horror and disorder. The Highlanders turned the abandoned French guns on the retreating enemy; the English and Prussians fired on each other, for a few minutes their cavalry met in a headlong charge. Along the main road, and far on either side streamed a torrent of panic-stricken men pursued by the allied cavalry.

At Decoster's house, 500 yards behind the original French lines, the Emperor drew up two battalions of the Guard who had not previously come under fire; these were the two battalions of the 1st Regiment of Grenadiers of the Old Guard, the *élite* of the *élite*. On horseback, within the first square, was Napoleon himself, still hoping that the fierce resistance he could expect from the Guard would be sufficient to stem the rout. For a while the two squares stood their ground, beset on all sides. The French who tried to seek refuge in the squares were driven off with bayonets and musket fire. Attacked by cannon, and mounting numbers of enemy cavalry and infantry, the Emperor ordered the withdrawal, and the *Grenadiers* marched slowly away before a running assault which from time to time they halted to drive off. Ahead of them rode the Emperor, Soult, Drouot, Bertrand and Lobau, and a handful of cavalry. At Le Caillou the party met the battalion of *Chasseurs* of the Old Guard left in charge of the Imperial baggage. Instructed by the Emperor to join him, the battalion set off down the road while Napoleon and his companions rode slowly by the side of the column. Some hundreds of yards in the rear the *Grenadiers* continued their journey at a normal pace and in excellent order, resisting the successive attacks of the Prussian cavalry so firmly that at last their pursuers gave up the struggle to go in search of easier prey. About a mile and a half from Genappe the commander of the *Grenadiers* was able to break up the squares and resume the march in column. Presently the Emperor left the *Chasseurs* and galloped forward to examine the possibilities of holding up the Prussians in front of the village and rallying his army there.

At a quarter-past nine that evening Blücher and Wellington met in front of La Belle Alliance; not far away the two squares of the Grenadiers of the Old Guard were still holding their position. The Prussian commander reached La Belle Alliance with Bülow's corps, and Wellington came from La Haye Sainte with the rear of his army. As the troops of the two armies met in what had been the French lines the Prussians broke into slow time and their bands played *God save the King*. Wellington and Blücher greeted each other as the victor, and Blücher suggested that La Belle Alliance would make an appropriate name for the battle. The Duke, preferred to give it the name of his headquarters, at Waterloo. After a brief consultation it was agreed that the Prussians should continue the pursuit. Blücher summoned his corps commanders and instructed them to "pursue the enemy as long as they had a man and a horse to stand." Gneisenau, his Chief of Staff, joined the cavalry of the Prussian vanguard to hasten the chase.

The Emperor reached Genappe only to find that there was no hope of halting the enemy. The village consisted of little more than a long winding street, ending at a bridge only eight feet wide across the Dyle. The long approaches to the bridge were packed by fugitives struggling to force a path for themselves through the overturned and abandoned vehicles. Soon movement virtually ceased along the street and for hundreds of yards behind the crossing the dense crowd of troops became more and more closely packed as those behind them attempted to push forwards.

Some tried to clear a passage with the use of their musket butts, the cavalry spurred their horses into the mass of men in front of them. Pressure met increased resistance. Bayonets and sabres were used, firing broke out, and the dead and wounded fell to the ground to encumber the living still more. The bridge these thousands of terrified men were killing one another to cross, led over a stream which was nowhere more than ten feet wide and three feet deep, and was impassable to wheeled traffic only because the banks were too steep. To the left and right of the village there was still ample ground leading to the Dyle. When the Prussians approached, impeded by only the three battalions of the Old Guard, still withdrawing in good order, the jam ended in an enormous mass vainly pushing and struggling outside the village itself. At the outskirts of Genappe the Guard broke their ranks to skirt the village by the east, a movement they executed without difficulty because the Prussians concentrated on the motionless herd before the bridge. Only when they saw their comrades falling beneath the Prussian lances did the fugitives find a way of escape by following the route the Guard had taken. The Prussian cavalry cut a path through Genappe, almost capturing the Emperor, who had taken over an hour to make his way along the street, and who was about to cross the bridge in his carriage, which shortly before had been discovered amongst the abandoned vehicles. Horses were being brought to harness to the coach when the Prussians' shouts were heard, and hastily descending from his carriage, the Emperor mounted his horse once more and galloped out of Genappe with his few companions as the enemy cavalry paused to plunder the Imperial carriage.

Blücher halted at Genappe, where he spent the night surrounded by the exhausted men of Bülow's corps. Zieten and Pirch's corps had not yet reached Le Caillou, and beyond Genappe Gneisenau conducted the pursuit with only the Uhlans and a couple of battalions of infantry. Before this force of 4,000 tired but exhilarated men 40,000 French fled with mounting despair. "It was a regular hunt," Gneisenau recorded, "a hunt by moonlight." The fugitives had lost all discipline, all self-possession; men from a hundred units marched in inextricable confusion, many of them had thrown away their arms, and if anyone had given orders, they would not have been obeyed. The Prussian cavalry ranged far and wide over the countryside in small bands, flushing weary soldiers from their bivouacs and driving them on into the night to spread the alarm among others who had thought it safe to halt. The panic, the desperation, the suicide of wounded men who dared not face capture, were very largely the fugitives' own making; had a few hundred banded together to resist the Uhlans the pursuit would have come to an abrupt halt.

The French continued their flight through the night, passing Quatre Bras, where in the moonlight lay the thousands who had fallen on the 16th, naked and unburied, stripped even of their shirts by the Belgian peasants. At the stream of Gemioncourt, where many paused briefly to slake their thirst, dead bodies drifted past the living. It was not until he had passed Frasnes that Gneisenau called off the chase; he had with him fewer than 2,000 men and horses who had been in the field for over twenty hours.

9

Aftermath

FROM LA BELLE ALLIANCE Wellington rode back slowly over
the battlefield to his headquarters in the inn at Waterloo, a solitary
figure followed at a distance by a handful of staff officers. He ate
some supper with those of his staff who had survived, and before
retiring, ordered Dr. Hume to bring him the casualty list early
on the next day, so that he could include it in his despatch. The
dying Sir Alexander Gordon had been brought to the inn, and the
Duke turned his bed over to him, going himself to lie down in
another room, wrapped in his cloak.

At five the next morning Dr. Hume brought in the list of
casualties, placing it silently by the sleeping Wellington. When
Hume returned the Duke was awake and up, and on his face, still
covered with the grime and dust of the previous day, the Doctor
saw the traces of tears. Before he left for Brussels to supervise the
provisioning of the army and the care of the wounded, Wellington
wrote his momentous despatch:

> "My Lord,
>   Bonaparte having collected the first, second, third, fourth and
> sixth corps of the French army, and the imperial guards, and
> nearly all the cavalry . . .
>   Your Lordship will observe, that such a desperate action could
> not be fought, and such advantages could not be gained without
> great loss; and I am sorry to say that ours has been immense. . . .
>   It gives me the greatest satisfaction to assure your Lordship,
> that the army never, upon any occasion, conducted itself bet-
> ter. . . ."

The dead and wounded in the English army numbered over
15,000, or almost one in four. The Prussians had lost 7,000, a
measure of their contribution to the victory, and the French, for
whom only approximate figures can be given, 25,000, in addition

to 8,000 prisoners and 220 guns. "Never did I see such a pounding match", wrote Wellington to his old friend Lord Beresford. "Both were what the boxers call gluttons. Napoleon did not manœuvre at all. He just moved forward in the old style, in columns, and was driven off in the old style. . . . " "In all my life", the Duke told his brother, "I have not experienced such anxiety, for I must confess that I have never been so close to defeat." Not far from the village the heaps of dead and wounded on the battlefield bore witness to the fierceness of the struggle; the margin of success had indeed been small. "The 27th Regiment (Inniskillings)", recorded Kincaid, "were lying literally dead in square." A frontal attack of many hours over a narrow space produced "more the appearance of a breach carried by assault than an extended field of battle", a cavalry officer wrote of the slopes from Hougoumont to La Haye Sainte. "The immediate neighbourhood of Hougoumont", says Mercer's *Journal*, "was more thickly strewn with corpses than most other parts of the field—the very ditches were full of them."

Some regiments had been reduced to a few companies. Almost the whole of the Duke's staff had been killed or wounded, and his own survival unscathed was one of the more remarkable features of the battle, for he had moved all day from one threatened point to another, directing and encouraging his men. "When a cannon-shot took off Lord Fitzroy Somerset's right arm", writes Maxwell, the Duke's biographer,

> "he was riding with his left arm touching the Duke's right. Again, when Lord Uxbridge lost his leg, the cannon shot which struck him passed first over the withers of Copenhagen. 'By God! I've lost my leg', cried Uxbridge. 'Have you, by God?' was all the Duke's reply!* De Lancey also received his mortal wound from a cannon shot when riding by the Duke's side; and his mind must have been more or less than human had he shown no sense of gratitude for the number and narrowness of his escapes. Nothing is rarer in the vast correspondence than appeals, or even references to the Almighty, though it cannot be denied that he often swore by His name; but at 3 a.m. on the morning of the battle, writing to Lady Frances Webster† to tell her that she might

---

* The Duke's terseness has been attributed not so much to preoccupation (the general advance had been ordered) as coldness. Uxbridge, his brother-in-law, had recently been notably unfaithful to his wife.

† "Lady Frances Webster was a very pretty woman, the wife of an officer in the 9th Light Dragoons." (Maxwell.)

remain in Brussels in perfect safety, after enumerating the chief losses he had sustained, he added, 'The finger of Providence was upon me, and I escaped unhurt.'"*

Nearly the whole of Wellington's army had taken part in the general advance at the end of the day, and when he halted his troops at La Belle Alliance, they lay down to rest among the deserted bivouacs in what had been the French rear lines. Mercer's battery slept where they had fought, and to this we owe the best description of the field the night after the battle:

"I found (them) preparing to go supperless to bed—the two remaining officers, the non-commissioned officers and men having all got together in a heap, with some painted covers spread under and others drawn over them—at a distance from our guns, &c., the neighbourhood of which, they said, was too horrible to think of sleeping there. For my part, after standing all day amongst these horrors, I felt no squeamishness about sleeping amongst them; so pulling down the painted cover of a limber over the footboard in the manner of a tent roof, I crept under it, and endeavoured to sleep. The cramped situation in which I lay, and the feverish excitement of my mind, forbade, however, my obtaining that sound and refreshing sleep so much needed—I only dozed. From one of these dozes I awoke about midnight, chilled and cramped to death from the awkward doubled-up position imposed upon me by my short and narrow bed. So up I got to look around and contemplate a battlefield by the pale moonlight. The night was serene and pretty clear; a few light clouds occasionally passing across the moon's disc, and throwing objects into transient obscurity, added considerably to the solemnity of the scene. . . . Here and there some poor wretch, sitting up amidst the countless dead, busied himself in endeavours to stanch the flowing stream with which his life was fast ebbing away. Many whom I saw so employed that night were, when morning dawned, lying stiff and tranquil as those who had departed earlier. From time to time a figure would half raise itself from the ground, and then, with a despairing groan, fall back again. Others, slowly and painfully rising, stronger, or having less deadly hurt, would stagger away with uncertain steps across the field in search of succour. Many of them I followed with my gaze until lost in the obscurity of distance; but many, alas! after staggering a few paces, would sink again on the ground, probably to rise no more. It was heartrending—and yet I gazed! Horses, too there were to claim our pity—mild, patient, enduring. Some lay on the ground with their entrails hanging out, and yet they lived. These would occasionally

---

* When the question of publication of this letter arose, in 1838, Wellington asked that names should be suppressed, and "The finger of Providence" omitted.

attempt to rise, but like their human bed-fellows, quickly falling back again, would lift their poor heads, and, turning again a wistful gaze at their side, lie quietly down again, to repeat the same until strength no longer remained, and then, their eyes gently closing, one short convulsive struggle closed their sufferings. One poor animal excited painful interest—he had lost, I believe, both his hind legs; and there he sat the long night through on his tail, looking about, as if in expectation of coming aid, sending forth, from time to time, long and protracted melancholy neighing. Although I knew that killing him at once would be mercy, I could not muster courage even to give the order. Blood enough I had seen shed during the last six-and-thirty hours, and sickened at the thought of shedding more. There, then, he still sat when we left the ground, neighing after us, as if reproaching our desertion of him in the hour of need.

"At length I again crept into my cell, and again slept by fits and starts, until the first blush of day reddened the eastern sky, and aroused us all to new exertion. As I emerged from under my cover a shudder crept over me, when the stronger light of day enabled me to see the corpse of one of my drivers lying mangled and bloody beneath my lair."

Lieutenant-Colonel Ponsonby's experiences after being wounded in a cavalry charge should not be taken as typical; he was more fortunate than many of the wounded in that he was not killed by the troops, English as well as Prussian, who roamed over the field at nightfall, stripping the fallen of their valuables. Of course, many more of the French wounded were murdered by the pillagers in search of a quick haul, than those of the allied army, but even for them the danger of surviving the battle only to be murdered by the criminal privates of both Blücher's and Wellington's armies was a very real one. Another English officer who passed the night on the field describes how he witnessed the death of a neighbour, a young English ensign, whose legs had been crushed by a gun-carriage, killed by a Prussian infantryman for his reluctance to surrender a trinket; and how he himself was saved from a similar fate by a couple of English soldiers, who shot the Prussian, and stripped him in his turn. They apologised for not being able to carry him to shelter and assistance on the grounds that they dare not betray their absence from their regiment, which had bivouacked on the other side of the field. This witness, like the others who survived to tell the tale, mentioned the cold of the night and his raging thirst as the worst of his sufferings.

Ponsonby was fortunate that his exposure ended so soon, although it must have seemed an eternity to him. Many of the allied wounded of lower rank spent two nights and a day, some even longer, without receiving assistance. The wonder is, that they recovered at all. "In the thick of the fight", writes Ponsonby,

"I was almost instantly disabled in both my arms, losing first my sword, and then my rein; and, followed by a few of my men who were presently cut down, no quarter being asked or given, I was carried along by my horse, till, receiving a blow from a sabre, I fell senseless on my face to the ground. Recovering, I raised myself a little to look round, being at that time in a condition to get up and run away, when a lancer, passing by, cried out, '*Tu n'es pas mort, coquin!*' and struck his lance through my back. My head dropped, the blood gushed into my mouth, a difficulty of breathing came on and I thought all was over. Not long after, a skirmisher stopped to plunder me, threatening my life: I directed him to a small side-pocket in which he found three dollars, all I had; but he continued to threaten, tearing open my waistcoat, and leaving me in a very uncomfortable posture.

"But he was no sooner gone, than an officer bringing up some troops, and happening to halt where I lay, stooped down, and addressing me, said, he feared I was badly wounded. I answered that I was, and expressed a wish to be moved to the rear. He said it was against orders to remove even their own men; but that, if they gained the day (and he understood that the Duke of Wellington was killed, and that six of our battalions had surrendered), every attention in his power should be shown me. I complained of thirst, and he held his brandy bottle to my lips, directing one of his soldiers to lay me straight on my side, and place a knapsack under my head: they then passed on into action, soon perhaps to want, though not to receive, the same assistance; and I shall never know to whose generosity I was indebted, as I believe, for my life.

"By and by, another skirmisher came up, a fine young man, full of ardour, loading and firing: he knelt down and fired over me many times, conversing with me very gaily all the while: at last he ran off, saying, '*Vous serez bien aise d'apprendre que nous allons nous retirer. Bonjour, mon ami.*' It was dusk, when two squadrons of Prussian cavalry crossed the valley in full trot, lifting me from the ground, and tumbling me about must cruelly.

"The battle was now over, and the groans of the wounded all around me, became more and more audible: I thought the night would never end. About this time I found a soldier lying across my legs, and his weight, his convulsive motions, his noises, and the air issuing through a wound in his side, distressed me greatly; the last circumstance most of all, as I had a wound of the same nature myself. It was not a dark night, and the Prussians were wandering about to plunder: many of them stopped to look at me as they passed; at last one of them stopped to examine me: I told him that I was a British officer, and had been already plundered. He did not however desist, and pulled me about roughly.

"An hour before midnight, I saw a man in an English uniform, coming towards me; he was, I suspected, on the same errand. I spoke instantly, telling him who I was: he belonged to the 40th, and had missed his regiment. He released me from the dying soldier, took up a sword, and stood over me as sentinel. Day broke, and at six o'clock in the morning a messenger was sent to Hervé: a cart came for me, and I was conveyed to the village of Waterloo, and laid in the bed, as I afterwards understood from which Gordon had just been carried out. I had received seven wounds; a surgeon slept in my room, and I was saved by excessive bleeding."

Mercer's *Journal* entry for the morning of the 19th of June deserves quotation at length; it is full of information about the tasks of a battery commander struggling to put his force into order to continue the campaign, and throws a great deal of light on the conditions which prevailed on a Napoleonic battlefield when the shouting was over, and the chroniclers of *la gloire* have gone. Mercer's battery left to join the army at three that afternoon, and accompanied the allied armies to Paris, going into action, although of a minor kind, on the way. If he and his men went so long without food or drink it may be imagined how much longer the thousands of wounded, scattered over an area of 8 square miles, were obliged to wait for even these elementary comforts. Helpers at first were few, and most of the wells too polluted for use. Even the active were lucky to find uncontaminated sources. The suffering inflicted by the lack of water is vividly suggested by Ensign Leeke. "On the other side of the fire-place" (in a cottage near the field, the day after the battle),

"on a bed or mattress, lay a poor fellow belonging to the grenadiers of the French Guard. He had, I thought, a fatal wound from which the bowels protruded. When he saw one of our men washing the wounds of a hussar, he begged that he would bring the water to him also; and on this being done, he eagerly seized the basin, and quenched his burning thirst by drinking deeply of bloody water which it contained."

Mercer's opinion of the Belgian peasants and the way they treated the French wounded makes surprising reading; no one who has visited this part of Belgium would imagine it possible that the character of its people should have changed so much in so comparatively short a time. The behaviour of their forbears is a welcome reminder that the twentieth century has not after all a monopoly of violence and brutality, and also a measure of the changes that have overtaken country life since the industrial revolution; for the attitude of the poorest Belgian townspeople was vastly more generous.

The two Irish light infantrymen who alienated Mercer may be taken as representative of only the worst type of Irish ne'er-do-wells who found a home in the English army. The misdeeds of the Irish are a constant theme of chroniclers of the Peninsular army, and provide a strange contrast to the reputation of the Scots, who enlisted from much the same reasons, poverty and unemployment, and yet who were given an excellent character, both off the field and on it—at Waterloo the Scots regiments distinguished themselves particularly. No doubt the explanation lies in the differing political climates of the two countries; any patriotic Scotsman would be prepared to join the army, few decent Irishmen could have been willing to enlist in the ranks of what was in effect an army of occupation.

> "Our first care . . . was to muster the remaining force, to disentangle our carriages from each other, and from the dead and dying animals with which they were encumbered. Many sound or only slightly wounded horses, belonging to the different corps of both armies, were wandering about the field. Of these we caught several in the course of the morning, and thus collected, with what remained of our own fit for work, sufficient to horse four guns, three ammunition waggons, and the forge. Of men we had nearly enough for these at reduced numbers, so we set to work equipping ourselves without delay. Although supplies of ammunition had been sent to us during the action, yet little remained. The expenditure had been enormous. A return had been called for yesterday evening just as we were lying down to rest, but fatigued as we all were, it was impossible to give this correctly. As near as I could ascertain, we must have fired nearly 700 rounds per gun. Our harness, etc., was so cut to pieces, that but for the vast magazines around us from which we could pick and choose, we should never have got off the field. . . . The scene was now far from solitary; for numerous groups of peasants were moving about busily employed stripping the dead, and perhaps finishing those not quite so. Some of these men I met fairly staggering under the enormous load of clothes, etc., they had collected. Some had firearms, swords, etc., and many had large bunches of

crosses and decorations; all seemed in high glee, and professed unbounded hatred of the French.

"... Wandering towards the Charleroi road I stumbled on a whole regiment of British infantry fast asleep, in columns of divisions, wrapped in their blankets, with their knapsacks for pillows. Not a man was awake. There they lay in regular ranks, with the officers and sergeants in their places, just as they would stand when awake. Not far from these, in a little hollow beneath a white thorn, lay two Irish light-infantry men sending forth such howlings and wailings, and oaths and execrations, as were shocking to hear. One of them had his leg shot off, the other a thigh smashed by a cannon-shot. They were certainly pitiable objects, but their vehement exclamations, etc., were so strongly contrasted with the quiet resolute bearing of hundreds, both French and English, around them, that it blunted one's feelings considerably.

"I tried in vain to pacify them; so walked away amidst a volley of abuse as a hardhearted wretch who could thus leave two poor fellows to die like dogs. What could I do? All, however, though in more modest terms, craved assistance; and every poor wretch begged most earnestly for water. Some of my men had discovered a good well of uncontaminated water at Hougoumont, and filled their canteens; so I made several of them accompany me and administer to the most craving in our immediate vicinity. Nothing could exceed their gratitude, or the fervent blessings they implored on us for this momentary relief. The French in general particularly grateful.... Many begged me to kill them at once, since they would a thousand times rather die by the hand of a soldier than be left at the mercy of those villainous Belgic peasants. Whilst we stood by them, several would appear consoled and become tranquil; but the moment we attempted to leave, they invariably renewed the cry, '*Ah, Monsieur, tuez moi donc! Tuez moi, pour l'amour de Dieu!*' etc., etc. It was in vain I assured them carts would be sent to pick them all up. Nothing would reconcile them to the idea of being left.... 'But the moment you go, those vile peasants will first insult, then cruelly murder us.' This, alas! I knew, was but too true. One Frenchman I found in a far different humour—an officer of lancers, and desperately wounded; a strong square-built man, with reddish hair and speckled complexion. When I approached him he appeared suffering horribly—rolling on his back, uttering loud groans. My first impulse was to raise and place him in a sitting posture; but, the moment he was touched, opening his eyes and seeing me, he became perfectly furious. Supposing he mistook my intention, I addressed him in a soothing tone, begging he would allow me to render what little assistance was in my power. This only seemed to irritate him the more; and on my presenting him the canteen with water, he dashed it from him with such a passionate gesture and emphatic '*Non!*' that I saw there was no use in teasing, and therefore reluctantly left him. Returning to our position, I was forcibly struck by the immense heap of bodies of men and horses which distinguished it even at a distance; indeed, Sir Augustus Frazer told me the other day, at Nivelles, that in riding over the field, '*he could plainly distinguish the position of G troop from the opposite height by the dark mass which, even at that distance, formed a remarkable feature in the field.*'

"The trees all about Hougoumont were most woefully cut and splintered, both by cannon-shot and musketry. The courts of the Château presented a spectacle more terrible even than any I had yet seen. A large barn had been set on fire, and the conflagration had spread to the offices, and even to the main building. Here numbers, both of French and English, had perished in the flames, and their blackened swollen remains lay scattered about in all directions. Amongst this heap of ruins and misery many poor devils yet remained alive, and were sitting up endeavouring to bandage their wounds. Such a scene of horror, and one so sickening, was surely never witnessed.

"... I now began to feel somewhat the effects of my long fast in a most unpleasant sense of weakness and an inordinate craving for food, which there were no means of satisfying. My joy, then, may be imagined when, returning to our bivouacs, I found our people returned from Lillois, and, better still, that they had brought with them a quarter of veal which they had found in a muddy ditch, of course in appearance then filthy enough. What was this to a parcel of men who had scarcely eaten a morsel for three days? In a trice it was cut up, the mud having been scraped off with a sabre, a fire kindled and fed with lance-shafts and musket stocks; and old Quartermaster Hall, undertaking the cooking, proceeded to fry the dirty lumps in the lid of a camp-kettle."

At three Mercer's troops set off along the Nivelles road to rejoin the army.

In Brussels and the neighbouring towns immense efforts were made to collect the wounded and relieve their suffering. The rudimentary medical services of the allied armies were, of course, swamped from the beginning, and despite the assistance of the widespread voluntary services which sprang into being, the solution of so vast a problem was beyond the resources of the period. There was no lack of generosity and good will; the first women appeared on the field the morning after the battle, to be met by a sight calculated to deter the bravest as well as the most charitable. Sightseers arrived as well, just as no doubt they would appear were there a similar spectacle to be viewed today. All witnesses agree to the great exertions made by the inhabitants of Brussels to comfort the wounded. Many wealthy people gave up their houses to casualties from both armies, and Miss Charlotte Eaton describes the sacrifices made by the poorer members of the population to provide shelter, food, spirits, and above all, linen to serve as dressings, for the thousands of wounded who survived the night or nights they had passed on the field, and the 9 miles' jolting in unsprung carts over primitive roads to the capital. So great was the task, however, that even after a month had passed, we read that the churches near Waterloo were still full of wounded. The death rate in the hospitals was very high, and many parents came from England only to witness the last hours of their sons or attend their funerals. The inquisitive acquired funds of stories of total amputations and death agonies. The charitable spent weeks of labour and sympathy on men with whom they could not communicate; the Highlanders were made much of. Whatever may have passed on the battlefield, the scenes in the streets and houses of Brussels during the month that followed outdid in poignancy and horror. Very unwillingly, the peasants in the neighbourhood of Waterloo were pressed into burying the dead, an enormous task in itself.

In Jones's *Battle of Waterloo* are printed Extracts from the *Journal of a Gentleman* which give much of the atmosphere:

"July 19. . . . Went to the hospitals, and saw at the doors prodigious crowds of females, waiting to administer succour to the wounded: officers and privates were found lying indiscriminately together, but very clean; females of rank attending them with surprising zeal. Saw soldiers slightly wounded in the field, using the French cuirasses as frying pans, to dress their victuals.

July 20. Visited another hospital, containing 420 wounded, half English and half French, all were taken care of, and very clean. They had all port wine and strong soups; but many were in a dying state, others the sight quite gone. Returning, witnessed a shocking sight, i.e. the dead drawn along by fish hooks; they were going to be buried in the fields by the peasants.

July 21. Visited the field of battle, and saw scattered about prodigious quantities of broken swords, spears, saddles, bridles, caps, all cut in pieces. Picked up two crosses of the Legion of Honour and an iron cross of Prussia. Saw vast numbers of cuirasses taken out of the water, into which they were thrown by the peasants for concealment, and afterwards sold for two francs each. Met waggons full of wounded, crying out from extreme suffering. The water everywhere quite red. There were 20,000 wounded at one time in Brussels. All the wells at Waterloo spoiled by throwing

men into them. Churches still full of wounded. No inhabitants
around Waterloo. We took a large quantity of camphor with us,
as a preventive against infection. Were much annoyed by the
incalculable swarms of carrion flies, preying on the carcasses of
the horses which still lie unburied. Owing to the dry weather, the
ground cracks or opens, and as the bodies of the men buried are
not above a foot below the surface, they may still be seen in many
places. The Prussians obliged the peasants to bury the dead at the
point of the bayonet; many were put to death for refusing. Since,
horses and men have been burnt together."

Although Miss Charlotte Eaton visited Waterloo a few days
before the last writer, she seems on this occasion at least to have
been more aware of the dead than the living. Possibly her escorts
took her on a path which skirted the shelters of the wounded.
She shared her generation's taste for the circumstantial and pathetic
detail:

"On top of the ridge in front of the British position, on the left of
the road, we traced a long line of tremendous graves, or rather
pits, into which hundreds of dead had been thrown as they had
fallen in their ranks. . . . The effluvia which arose from them,
even beneath the open canopy of heaven, was horrible; and the
pure west wind of summer, as it passed us, seemed pestiferous,
so deadly was the smell that in many places pervaded the field.
In many places the excavations made by the shells had thrown up
the earth all around them; the marks of horses' hoofs, that had
plunged ankle deep in clay, were hardened in the sun: and the feet
of men, deeply stamped in the ground, left traces of where many
a deadly struggle had been. The ground was ploughed up in
several places with the charge of the cavalry, and the whole field
was literally covered with soldiers' caps, shoes, gloves, belts, and
scabbards, broken feathers battered into the mud, remnants of
tattered scarlet cloth, bits of fur and leather, black stocks and
havresacs belonging to the French soldiers, buckles, packs of
cards, books, and innumerable papers of every description. I
picked up a volume of *Candide*; a few sheets of sentimental love-
letters, evidently belonging to some French novel; and many
other pages of the same publication were flying over the field in
much too muddy a state to be touched. One German Testament,
not quite so dirty as many that were lying about, I carried with
me nearly the whole day;—printed French military returns, muster rolls, love-letters and washing bills; illegible songs, scattered
sheets of military music, epistles without number in praise of
'l'Empereur, le Grand Napoléon', and filled with the most confident anticipations of victory under his command, were strewed
over the field which had been the scene of his defeat. The quantities of letters and of blank sheets of dirty writing paper were so
great that they literally whitened the face of the earth."

Although he escaped from Genappe only a matter of yards ahead of his pursuers, the Emperor rode on to Quatre Bras through the crowds of fugitives from his army still thinking that the rout might be halted, the scattered troops remustered, and somehow, miraculously, the situation retrieved. For twenty years he had been accustomed to achieving what he had willed, and the habit was too strong to be broken now. Throughout his journey back to the capital, and even after his abdication, the Emperor's mind was full of unrealisable plans, which fell to pieces as soon as they had been broached, only to be replaced by further flights of fantasy. Yet when his advisers pointed out the impossibility of any of his schemes, he did not resist; and when his brother, in Paris, urged him to make another stand for his throne, Napoleon poured cold water on the idea. It seems as if the Emperor's proposals, for all that some of them were put on paper and addressed to the Council of State or later the Provisional Government, were almost a private game to satisfy the craving for activity and decision, and so deaden the hurt of the destruction of his world. Napoleon reached Quatre Bras towards one o'clock in the morning of Monday, the 19th of June. He dismounted while some of his staff were sent to gather information about the forces available for action. A few of the *grenadiers* of the Guard lit a fire, by which the Emperor stood, alone and silent, his arms folded, staring in the direction of Waterloo. That is how one passer-by saw him; others recognised the Emperor by the light of the fire, and hurried on, skirting the tiny bivouac. Napoleon insisted that Grouchy should be informed of the loss of the battle and given instructions to extricate himself from his exposed position. Soult thought this unnecessary; by now Grouchy must have been defeated and his forces dispersed. The Emperor had his way, and a horseman was despatched to make his path through the enemy territory as best he could with orders to the Marshal for a retreat to the Sambre. The officer was fortunate enough to reach Grouchy's quarters by half-past ten the next morning, where he retailed his story of disaster and was thought for a while, by some of his listeners, in the absence of any papers to substantiate himself or his message, to be a spy. Grouchy's force was still intact, and he was preparing to march in the direction of Brussels, in accordance with the Emperor's plan of campaign.

The history of Grouchy's successful march from his position behind hostile forces of 150,000 men is too little known, for it is an impressive record of skill, courage and determination which serves as a reminder, if reminder were necessary, that Grouchy was not 'the man who betrayed Napoleon at Waterloo' of popular myth. No doubt, as General Fuller observes, if Grouchy had shown the same qualities on the 18th that he did during the days which followed, the result of the battle would have been far different.

Napoleon was still waiting by the fire for news of the reinforcements he hoped were in the neighbourhood when one of the officers he had sent to look for them returned to report that the sound of musketry and a drum beating the advance could be heard not far off. The Emperor and his companions had no more idea than the men who were streaming past the cross-roads how small were the Prussian forces still pursuing them; the drummer who was causing so much panic amongst the fugitives was a young fellow perched on a horse taken from Napoleon's carriage at Genappe. Even had they known, there were no means of finding troops to call a halt to the enemy's advance. The cavalcade set off for Charleroi, which they reached at dawn.

The Emperor crossed the bridge at Charleroi and stopped outside the town. It was not long before Charleroi became the scene of the same confusion and indiscipline that had been witnessed at Genappe; and with far less excuse. The town was crowded with baggage trains and carriages, the prisoners and the 27 guns taken at Ligny. There were large numbers of casualties from the 16th and 17th and these had been joined by the wounded who had been carried from Waterloo during the first hours of the battle. Early on the 19th the leading fugitives from the Prussian army arrived. Their behaviour gave fresh strength to the old adage that the French were more than men in the attack, but less than women in retreat. Although the Prussians did not approach the town before mid-day, few people acted calmly, or considered the very strong possibility that Blücher's men had been obliged to halt to eat, rest and regroup. All order vanished from Charleroi hours before the first Prussian cavalry caught sight of the outskirts. Difficulties began when a number of carriages were involved in an accident on the bridge; before long the ensuing jam stretched the length of the bridge and for a considerable distance along its approaches. A modicum of organisation and time would have been all that was necessary to clear the obstruction and set the traffic moving again, but the fugitives had carried the seeds of panic with them, far in advance of the Prussian vanguard. Those on foot gave the drivers no chance to extricate their vehicles; they made their way over the halted waggons and carriages and pressed on to the south in as much disorder as if their pursuers were close behind them. Recognising the impossibility of taking the transport through, the officer in charge of the carriage carrying the state papers ordered his men to tear up and scatter the most important documents; the vehicles of the Treasury were in the same predicament, and here the expedient of distributing the bags of gold to the members of the escort was being adopted when shots were heard and cries of "The Prussians are here! Save yourselves!" went up, and in the resulting confusion, the chests were emptied and the contents lost. The plunderers had utilised the alarm created by the thirsty stragglers who had been loosing off their muskets into the barrels of wine and spirits which encumbered the streets, and added their cries to those who genuinely believed that the Prussians had arrived. The town was full of supplies, but the French got no more of them than they could obtain by putting their canteens to the leaking barrels or by spearing a loaf on their bayonets from the overturned waggons they passed. Along the main street streams of red wine ran into the Sambre.

An hour after his arrival at Charleroi the Emperor resumed his journey to Philippeville which he reached two hours later, at nine o'clock. Here he paused to issue orders for the rallying of the army, largely to be concentrated at Laon. Instructions were sent to commanders of depots and garrisons to revictual the stragglers who reached them, and to direct their march to join the rest of the army. The Emperor wrote his last Bulletin, and a number of letters which were sent post-haste to Paris. Leaving Soult in charge of the concentration of the army, Napoleon climbed into a carriage to continue his journey to Paris, where he had to appear as quickly as possible if he were to forestall his deposition at the hands of the Chambers and the intriguers headed by Fouché. By early evening the Imperial party were at Laon. Between ten and eleven that night they left the town, and their long journey ended at six in the morning of the 21st, when the Emperor entered the Elysée for the last time.

Although he had hurried back to avoid what had happened in 1814, when he had been overthrown while he was away from the centre of affairs at the head of his defeated army, Napoleon refused to carry out the coup d'état which alone could have ensured his continued control of affairs. Militarily the situation was an impossible one. Even if he collected the National Guard, the men in the depots, and the remnants of the army which had been defeated in Belgium, the allied forces would swamp them. Politically, his position was equally untenable. The governments of the coalition powers were certainly not going to tolerate his remaining on the throne, and the French politicians who had grudgingly acquiesced in his rule at the beginning of the Hundred Days had withdrawn their support on the news of Waterloo. Napoleon retained a surprisingly strong measure of popular approval; the radically-minded workers of the capital were ready to follow him still, but the Emperor baulked at the thought of starting what in effect would be a civil war, and one, moreover, which he would be bound to lose, and which would be fought as the allied armies entered France, thus ensuring the harshest of peace terms. The Emperor had been disturbed by the cries which had greeted his return to France in March. His political instincts abhorred the demands for measures against the Church and aristocracy. His love for power was not so strong that he was prepared to make himself a jacobin ruler; the very idea made nonsense of his political career. The groups and individuals who had supported his régime were now alienated from him, and he bowed to the inevitable when, on the day after his return, he abdicated in favour of his young son. Eight days had passed since the campaign of 1815 had opened.

Viewed in perspective, the entire Hundred Days seem little more realistic than the plans for a last defence of his throne which Napoleon made and rejected at the end of his second reign. In April 1814 the marshals themselves had joined with the men of affairs in insisting that they must dispense with Napoleon; if his presence on the throne meant that France must fight a Europe united in arms against her, then the Emperor had to go. The Bourbons were restored in his place, though not as absolute monarchs. The first Restoration was not popular with the mass of the army and the common people, but it scarcely shook the conviction of most of the Emperor's old lieutenants that they were better off without him. Some of the more loyal joined him again on his return, though none without doubts; many left the country with the exiled king or withdrew entirely from public life; the remainder judged it best to accept the *fait accompli* and try to dismantle as much as possible of the Emperor's old system, in case he should succeed in perpetuating his rule. Of those who remained, the more cynical and adroit, like Fouché, played a double game, intriguing with the exile while they served Napoleon. Fouché even made arrangements for a woman to leave the capital carrying letters containing details of the army's mobilisation; when she reached the frontier one of his agents was there to stop her.* Only Fouché could have played the game with such finesse, but his motives were common to most of the officials Napoleon left behind him in the capital when he went to meet the English and Prussians. When the Emperor returned, defeated, Fouché and his fellows had come into the open, united at least in their determination to be rid of him.

The allied armies continued their march towards Paris, the Prussians ahead of the English, who proceeded more slowly, possibly because they were less inspired by thoughts of revenge— they had not experienced French occupation—possibly because of the disorganisation which had been caused by their heavy losses at Waterloo. The elements of the French army which had been remustered fell back before the numerically superior enemy, their morale enfeebled by the Emperor's abdication. As the three armies approached Paris the French recovered to a great extent their will to fight and avenge themselves for their defeat at Waterloo. Their leaders were more aware of the hopelessness of such plans, although the possibilities of active resistance were seriously

---

* One of Napoleon's constant regrets at St. Helena was that he did not take advantage of his opportunity during the Hundred Days to have Fouché shot. But Fouché, like Talleyrand, was an even abler politician than Napoleon. The arch-intriguer's triumph was yet to come.

considered. The consequences of allied occupation and the terms of an imposed peace were not to be lightly dismissed.

In so fluid a political situation every solution was considered by one or other of the parties. Beyond the common agreement that Napoleon must go, it was hard to decide which arrangements would be best. On the 25th, four days after his abdication, Napoleon retired to Malmaison, where he had not been long before his fertile brain produced the last and most fantastic of his schemes. He wrote to Fouché's provisional government suggesting that the French state might be glad to make use of his skill as a general, and he offered his services in this capacity, mentioning the successes that might be won if he were placed at the head of the troops which could be found to oppose the invaders. The offer was rejected. The provisional government had been thoroughly relieved to get the fallen Emperor safely out of the capital to Malmaison, where they were careful to see that he was well protected from any "disaffected elements". They were even more pleased to agree to his departure for the western coast, whither Napoleon journeyed, debating the desirability of taking a boat for the United States. Early in July he surrendered himself to the commander of the *Bellerophon*, one of the blockading ships of the Royal Navy, and from which he wrote to the Prince Regent, throwing himself "on the mercy of his most constant and generous enemy".

Some of the allies thought that the ease with which the Emperor had been able to overthrow Louis XVIII and his government constituted sufficient grounds for ruling him out as the next occupant of the French throne. The remaining princes of the royal houses were considered. The idea of a French republic was mooted, but this did not recommend itself to a coalition of monarchies. The English government were convinced that only a return to legitimacy in the shape of Louis XVIII would do, and it must be concluded that this arrangement made more sense than any of the others in a particularly nonsensical situation. Their arguments were strengthened for their allies by reason of Wellington's victory and the heavy subsidies which had been paid to put the allied armies on the march.

Wellington's proclamation on crossing the French frontier made the English position quite clear. His forces were the allies of Louis

XVIII, and they had come to expel the usurper. The restored King marched with the rear of his powerful allies, whose support was by no means an unmixed blessing. The behaviour of the Prussians in particular so closely resembled that of an occupying army that it was not long before Louis had to protest against the wake of destruction they left behind them, and threatened to abandon his untenable situation. This, like so many of the difficulties which arose in the early months of the new régime, called for all the Duke's firmness and patience.

The King entered Cambrai behind the allied army on the 25th of June, the same day that Napoleon left Paris for Malmaison. Sergeant Wheeler of the 51st Light Infantry gave a spirited description of the occasion in one of his letters home. He had a clear sense of the reality behind politics, certainly behind French politics of the period, and in common with many of the English army, felt the sense of glamour about Napoleon. His admiration for the enemy commander provides a curious parallel with the prestige Rommel enjoyed amongst his opponents in the desert, although there, of course, the analogy ends:

> "The 25th [of June] we halted, and His pottle belly Majesty, Louis 18th, marched into the loyal town of Cambray. His Majesty was met by a deputation of his beloved subjects who received their father and their king with tears of joy. Louis blubbered over them like a big girl for her bread and butter, called them his children, told them a long rigmerole of nonsence about France, and his family, about his heart, how he had always remembered them in his prayers, and I don't know what. The presence of their good old fat King had a wonderful effect on their tender consciences, the air rent with their acclamations. The loyal and faithful soldiers of the Great Napoleon followed their example and surrendered the citadel to their beloved master Old Bungy Louis.
>
> "No doubt the papers will inform you how Louis 18th entered the loyal city of Cambray, how his loyal subjects welcomed their beloved king, how the best of monarchs wept over the sufferings of his beloved people, how the Citadel surrendered with acclamations of joy to the best of kings, and how his most Christian Majesty effected all this without being accompanied by a single soldier. But the papers will not inform you that the 4th Division and a brigade of Hanoverian Huzzars (red) were in readiness within half a mile of this faithful city, and if the loyal citizens had insulted their king, how it was very probably we should have bayoneted every Frenchman in the place. The people well knew this, and this will account for the sudden change in their

loyalty or allegiance from their *Idol Napoleon* (properly named) *the Great*, to an old bloated poltroon, the Sir John Falstaff of France."

On the 3rd of July Blücher entered Versailles. The Prussian forces were now a considerable distance from their allies, and the provisional government debated for a time whether to take advantage of the exposed and scattered positions the Prussians had adopted. The French army was eager and ready for action. The government was bound to consider whether any benefits might be gained for a victory over the invaders. Although there was every chance of short-term success, it was obvious that in the long run a victory could only result in fresh disasters, and the proposal was dropped. Negotiations were begun to settle the peaceful occupation of Paris and the withdrawal of the French forces in and around the city.

Fouché made the utmost use of his temporary bargaining power. Discussions were held, but made no great progress. Talleyrand, who had accompanied the King on his exile and his return, gave his advice on how to hasten the conclusion of the talks. Wellington leant the weight of his support to Talleyrand's proposal. At the start of the next meeting with the French representatives, Wellington addressed Fouché with the words: " . . . *Lisons un peu ce papier que tient Monsieur de Talleyrand*." Talleyrand held the patent appointing Fouché as Minister of Louis XVIII. Fouché had made his last coup; the arrangements for the occupation of Paris were soon concluded. One disgusted royalist recorded the remarkable scene as the lame Talleyrand, who himself had contrived to serve Louis XVI during the last years of the Ancien Régime, and each succeeding régime, the Assembly, the Republic, the Consulate, the Empire and the Restoration, hobbled on the arm of Fouché to conduct him to his new master—*le vice appuyé sur le crime*.

During the two days before the allies entered Paris the Emperor's last army set off to its final destination south of the Loire. Many of the regiments were reluctant to go without fighting, and it was with some difficulty that their commanders persuaded them to leave the city. In the weeks which followed the army was disbanded and it was a tribute to the skill with which the Ministry of War and the generals conducted the operation that the soldiers made

their way home without leaving behind them the trail of pillage
and violence across the countryside which usually accompanied
the rapid demobilisation of an army during the period.

On the 7th of July the allied armies entered Paris together.
"July 7th. Fine hot day", wrote Mercer in his *Journal*.

"Since early morning the road from Paris has been crowded with
people of all ages, sexes and conditions flocking to Arnouvilles
to greet their *beloved monarch*. The whole population seems to have
turned out, so continuous is the stream. Berlines, calèches, eques-
trians, and pedestrians, flow along without cessation or diminu-
tion of numbers. All are in their *habits de Dimanche*, and all gay and
merry. It is a perfect holiday, which all seem to enjoy without
alloy. I could scarcely persuade myself that the gay throng passing before me was the same that, after being accustomed for a
quarter of a century to look upon themselves as invincible, then
twice within a twelvemonth saw themselves humbled to the dust,
and those whom they had so long accustomed to trample on in
military possession of their capital, who were now hastening to
do homage to the family twice driven from their throne—and
who, in traversing the bivouacs of their conquerors, saw on all
sides the wreck and ruin of their own houses, fields and gardens;
—yet, nothing daunted, on they went, laughing, chatting, and
even singing, in the gayest of all possible moods. For them it was
a *jour de fête*, which they seemed determined to enjoy, no matter
what its origin. The smart dresses and lively colour contrasted
strongly with the dingy clothing, hardy embrowned visages,
and apathetic demeanour of our soldiery, who lounged at the
roadside, amused by the passing crowd. There were the members
of the Legislative Assembly in their embroidered uniforms, some
in carriages, some on horseback, others walking and looking
dignified; near them, perhaps, a group of pretty brunettes, with
brilliant black eyes and coquettishly arranged *cornetts*. Then
comes a national Guardsman with his blue and red uniform, with
white breeches and *brown-topped boots*, strutting along most conse-
quentially, a handkerchief in hand, which ever and anon he
applies to wipe the dust from his fair face. . . .

"In the afternoon I mounted Cossack and joined the throng.
There was no choice but to go at their pace, so completely filled
was the road. The easy, natural good-humoured manner in which
my companions, right and left, chatted and laughed with me, left
no room to feel oneself a foreigner, much less an enemy. We
were all 'hail fellow well met'. Occasional openings allowed me
from time to time to push on, and thus change my company.
There was, however, no difference between them in one respect—
I always found my new friends just as chatty and good-humoured
as those left behind.

"At Arnouvilles, still following the stream, I was swept into

199

the palace gardens, and found myself in the midst of a most gay *fête-champêtre*. All had come provided with a little basket, or something of the sort, and now, seated around a clean white cloth spread on the grass, numerous parties were enjoying at once the coolness and fragrance under the shade of fine trees or thickets of acacias, laburnums, syringas, &c., &c. Merry laughter, and an occasional ' *Vive le Roi!*' resounded on all sides, and was from time to time responded to more loudly by the crowd assembled without, all anxious to get a sight of their *new old King.*"

Mercer watched the procession which preceded the King.

"The royal carriages, drawn by post-horses, came next, and in outward appearance were little better than those of his majesty's guns. Louis was in the last carriage, and a dense cloud of pedestrians, with a plentiful admixture of British officers on horseback, closed the procession. I accompanied the throng as far as St. Denis, which took up a considerable time, since its movements were necessarily slow. No complimentary movement was made by our troops, although his majesty passed through the midst of us. The more curious crowded to the roadside, which was lined by them, but all in their fatigue-jackets, or even without any— but numbers remained at their occupations, or sitting smoking at a distance. The brigade of Highlanders alone cheered as the King passed through their bivouac. Why was this? Is there any connection between this and the protection afforded the Stuarts by the Bourbon family? Certain it is that the Highlanders alone cheered! The entrance to St. Denis was almost impossible, such was the multitude choking up the street, peasantry as well as citizens; and, as the royal carriages approached, they made the air ring with their shouts of ' *Vive le Roi!*' ' *Vivent les Bourbons!*' Only a short month ago, perhaps, these same people, and on this very spot, had shouted as lustily, ' *Vive l'Empereur!*' ' *Vive Napoléon!*' ' *A bas les Bourbons!*' etc., etc. I never felt prouder of being an Englishman! From Garges to St. Denis I kept close to the royal carriage, watching the countenance of his majesty in order to detect any emotion. He betrayed none. It was calm, serious, and unvarying in general, occasionally illumined by a faint smile as he returned salutations, but the smile was evanescent—very—and the features immediately resumed their calmness. Our troops seemed to attract considerable interest, particularly the Highlanders; and to every English officer he paid most marked attention, returning their salutes with eagerness and punctilio."

At the gates of Paris, Chabrol, the prefect of the Seine, addressed the King in a brief speech a phrase of which was to pass into history: "A hundred days have passed since the fatal moment when Your Majesty left his capital. . . . "

Appendixes

I. *Promotion of the Duke of Wellington*

Born	1st May 1769
Ensign	7th March 1787
Lieutenant	25th December 1787
Captain	20th June 1791
Major	30th April 1793
Lieutenant-Colonel	30th September 1793
Colonel	3rd May 1796
Major-General	29th April 1802
Lieutenant-General	25th April 1808
General, in Spain and Portugal	31st July 1811
Field-Marshal	21st June 1813

II. *Waterloo Prize Money*

	£	s.	d.
Commander-in-Chief	61,000	0	0
General officers	1,274	10	$10\frac{3}{4}$
Field officers and colonels	433	2	$4\frac{1}{4}$
Captains	90	7	$3\frac{3}{4}$
Subalterns	34	14	$9\frac{1}{2}$
Sergeants	19	4	4
Corporals, drummers and privates	2	11	4

Bibliography

AERTS, Winand, et WILMET, Léon. *18 juin 1815. Waterloo, l'attaque de la Garde. Les derniers carrés.* Bruxelles. 1904.

BAIN, Nicolson. *A Detailed Account of the Battles of Quatre Bras, Ligny and Waterloo,* 1816.

BATTY, Lieut.-Colonel Robert. *An Historical Sketch of the Campaign of 1815.* 2nd edition. 1820.

BEAMISH, Major N. L. *History of the King's German Legion.* 2 vols. 1832, 1837.

BECKE, Captain A. F. *Napoleon and Waterloo.* Revised edition. 1936.

BUGEAUD, Maréchal Thomas Robert. *Aperçus sur quelques détails de la guerre.* 3rd edition. 1846.

CHAMBRAY, Marquis de. *Oeuvres,* Vol. V. 1840.

CHENIER, L. J. Gabriel de. *Histoire de la vie militaire, politique et administrative du maréchal Davout.* 1866.

CHESNEY, Charles. *Waterloo Lectures: a study of the campaign of 1815.* 2nd edition. 1869.

COLIN, J. L. A. *L'Education militaire de Napoléon.* 1900.

— *La Tactique et la discipline dans les Armées de la Révolution.* 1902.

— *Les Transformations de la Guerre.* 1911.

— *Les Grandes Batailles de l'histoire.* 1915.

COTTON, Edward. *A Voice from Waterloo.* 3rd edition, 1849.

DROUET, Le Maréchal, Comte d'Erlon. *Vie Militaire écrite par lui-même.* 1844.

EATON, Charlotte. *Narrative of a residence in Belgium during the Campaign of 1815.* 1817.

ELLESMERE, The Earl of. *Personal Reminiscences of the Duke of Wellington.* 1903.

FARMER, G. *The Light Dragoon.* 1851.

FITCHETT, W. H. *Wellington's Men. Some Soldier Autobiographies.* 1900.

FOY, Le Général. *Histoire de la Guerre de la Péninsule.* Vol. I. 1827.

FRAZER, Colonel Sir Augustus. *Letters Written during the Peninsular and Waterloo Campaigns.* 1859.

— *Remarks on the Organisation of the Corps of Artillery in the British Service.* 1818.

FULLER, Major-General J. F. C. *The Decisive Battles of the Western World.* Vols. II and III. 1956.

GOURGAUD, Baron. *Campagne de 1815.* 1818.

GRONOW, Captain Rees Howell. *Reminiscences of Captain Gronow . . . being anecdotes of the camp, the court, and the clubs, at the close of the last war with France . . .* 1862.

— *Recollections and anecdotes: being a second series of Reminiscences . . .* 1863.

HARRIS, Rifleman. *Recollections of Rifleman Harris.* 1907.

HART, Captain B. H. Liddell. *The Ghost of Napoleon.* 1933.

HAY, Captain William. *Reminiscences . . . 1808–1815 under Wellington.* 1901.

HIME, Henry William Lovett. *The Origin of Artillery, etc.* 1915.

— *Gunpowder and Ammunition: their origin and progress.* 1904.

HOBHOUSE, John Cam. *The Substance of some Letters written from Paris during the Last Reign of the Emperor Napoleon.* 3rd edition. 2 vols. 1817.

BIBLIOGRAPHY

HOPE, Lieutenant James. *Letters from Portugal, Spain and France, etc.* Edinburgh. 1819.

HOUSSAYE, Henri. *1815.* 3 vols. 1895–1905.

JAMES, Lieut-Colonel W. H. *The Campaign of 1815, chiefly in Flanders.* 1908.

JANIN, E. F. *Campagne de Waterloo.* 1820.

JONES, George. *The Battle of Waterloo.* 1852.

KELLY, Christopher. *The Memorable Battle of Waterloo.* 1817.

KENNEDY, General Sir John Shaw. *Notes on the Battle of Waterloo.* 1865.

KINCAID, Captain Sir J. *Adventures in the Rifle Brigade.* 1929.

LACHOUQUE, Commandant Henry. *Le Secret de Waterloo.* 1952.

LAWRENCE, W. *The Autobiography of Sergeant William Lawrence.* 1856.

LEEKE, William. *The History of Lord Seaton's Regiment at the Battle of Waterloo, etc.* 2 vols., 1866, 1871.

LENIENT, E. *La Solution des énigmes de Waterloo.* 1915.

MALMESBURY, James Harris, First Earl of. *A Series of Letters of the First Earl of Malmesbury, his family and friends.* 2 vols. 1870.

MAXWELL, Sir Herbert. *The Life of Wellington.* 2 vols. 1899.

MERCER, General Cavalié. *Journal of the Waterloo Campaign.* 2 vols. 1870.

MORRIS, Sergeant Thomas. *Recollections of Military Service in 1813, 1814, and 1815.* 1845.

NAPOLEON. *Correspondance.* 1858–1869.
　　　　　Lettres Inédites de Napoléon Ier. 1897.
　　　　　Commentaires de Napoléon Ier. 1867.

NAVEZ, L. *La Campagne de 1815.* 2 vols. Bruxelles. 1910.

NEY, Joseph Napoléon, duc d'Elchingen. *Documents Inédits sur la Campagne de 1815.* 1840.

OMAN, C. W. C. *Wellington's Army 1809–1814.* 1912.

REGNAULT, Général Jean. *La Campagne de 1815: Mobilisation et Concentration.* 1935.

— *Une leçon de tactique. Revue Historique de l'Armée.* September 1951.

ROBERTSON, D. *The Journal of Sergeant D. Robertson.* Perth. 1842.

ROPES, J. C. *The Campaign of Waterloo.* 1893.

SAUVIGNY, Bertier de. *La Restauration.* 1955.

SIBORNE, William. *The Waterloo Campaign.* 1894.

SIBORNE, Major-General H. T. *Waterloo Letters.* 1891.

STANHOPE, Fifth Earl of. *Notes of Conversations with the Duke of Wellington. 1831–1851.* 1888.

STEVENSON, Sergeant John. *A Soldier in Time of War.* 1841.

TOMKINSON, Lieut-Colonel W. *The Diary of a Cavalry Officer in the Peninsular and Waterloo Campaigns.* 1894.

WARTENBURG, Count Yorck von. *Napoleon as a General.* 2 vols. 1902.

WELLINGTON. *Supplementary Despatches, Correspondence and Memoranda.* 1858–1865.

WHEELER, Private* William. *The Letters of Private Wheeler 1809–1828.* Edited, and with a foreword by Captain B. H. Liddell Hart. 1951.

WILKINSON, Spenser. *The French Army before Napoleon.* 1915. *The Rise of General Bonaparte.* 1930.

* Sergeant Wheeler at the time of Waterloo.

Index

The numerals in heavy type refer to the *figure numbers* of the illustrations